Washington Gladden

Ruling ideas of the present age

Washington Gladden

Ruling ideas of the present age

ISBN/EAN: 9783742894830

Hergestellt in Europa, USA, Kanada, Australien, Japan

Cover: Foto ©Thomas Meinert / pixelio.de

Manufactured and distributed by brebook publishing software
(www.brebook.com)

Washington Gladden

Ruling ideas of the present age

RULING IDEAS OF THE PRESENT AGE

BY

WASHINGTON GLADDEN

AUTHOR OF "APPLIED CHRISTIANITY," "TOOLS AND THE
MAN," "WHO WROTE THE BIBLE," ETC.

BOSTON AND NEW YORK
HOUGHTON, MIFFLIN AND COMPANY
The Riverside Press, Cambridge
1898

PREFACE.

By the will of the Hon. Richard Fletcher, a fund was committed to the trustees of Dartmouth College, the income of which was to be expended in obtaining and publishing, once in two years, a prize essay whose purpose it should be to impress on the minds of all Christians "*a solemn sense of their duty to exhibit in their godly lives and conversation the beneficent effects of the religion they profess, and thus increase the efficiency of Christianity in Christian countries, and recommend its acceptance to the heathen nations of the world.*"

In accordance with this provision the trustees asked for essays, in the year 1894, upon the question: "*In what ways ought the conception of personal life and duty to be modified?*" The essay which follows is the one to which the prize was awarded.

The title given to the volume was suggested, as most readers will know, by Canon Mozley's "Ruling Ideas in Early Ages." Not only is it needful to interpret the thought of past ages to the men of the present day, it seems also necessary to interpret the present to itself. The regulative truths which are working themselves out in the experience of every generation are often but imperfectly articulate, and it is a good service if one can help his neighbors to discern the meaning of the intellectual and ethical movements that are going on around them. This essay is a humble attempt at such an interpretation. It is not assumed that all the ruling ideas of the present age are here defined; but it is hoped that some of the more important among them have been pointed out.

W. G.

First Congregational Church,
Columbus, O., October 4, 1895.

CONTENTS.

I.

CHANGE YOUR MINDS.

Redemption must be wrought out, and is being wrought out, by living, present principles finding their way into the thoughts, hearts, actions of men. Redemption is an organic process, going on at this very time, and is to be judged in its own nature without passing beyond the hour. — JOHN BASCOM, *The Words of Christ*, Introduction.

Men are ruled by ideas: the military impulse is but an idea; and they may therefore be ruled by increasingly noble and just ideas. If the convictions and feelings incident to goodwill can be made forceful in their thoughts, all external expressions will conform to them, and conform to them with wonderful rapidity. Here, then, in ideas, is the truly constructive centre of human society. He only builds for the future who establishes, intensifies, and purifies the appropriate ideas. — *Ibid.*, pages 38, 39.

A ray of heavenly light traversing human life, the message of Christ has been broken into a thousand rainbow colors and carried in a thousand directions. It is the historical task of Christianity to assume with every age a fresh metamorphosis, and to be forever spiritualizing more and more her understanding of the Christ and of salvation. — AMIEL'S *Journal*, page 3.

RULING IDEAS OF THE PRESENT AGE.

I.

CHANGE YOUR MINDS.

THE first words of that Forerunner who came preaching in the wilderness of Judea were these: "Change your minds, for the kingdom of heaven is at hand." The coming of that kingdom is always a call to men to change their minds. A new conception of life and duty is the condition of entrance into the kingdom. We must be transformed before we can be naturalized; but we are transformed by the renewing of our minds, by getting new ideas of life and duty. The feelings, the choices, the habits, are also changed, but the foundation of it all is a new conception of the meaning of life.

The kingdom of heaven came, in the days of John the Baptist, only to those who changed their minds, and adopted its ruling principles as the law of their life. Just as fast and as far as the fundamental ideas of that kingdom were appropriated by men were its boundaries widened and its empire confirmed. The seat of this government is in candid minds and consenting wills. " The kingdom of God is within you."

This kingdom was coming while John was preaching in the wilderness, and while Jesus was speaking on the Mount of the Beatitudes. And ever since then the disciples of Christ have been offering the prayer, " Thy kingdom come." The prayer is answered, century by century and day by day. The kingdom does come. It continues to come, in stronger force, with wider sway, as the years go on. But how? Only as men change their minds, and give it freer entrance to their lives and larger authority over them.

The men who heard John speak changed

their minds about some things, and the kingdom of heaven came, in some partial measure, to them. They changed their minds about the sufficiency of the Jewish ritual. They saw that the formalities of the ceremonial worship were not enough; that they must do works meet for repentance. Religion, they had come to apprehend, was not a matter of form, but a matter of conduct. When this change in their habitual thinking had taken place, the kingdom of heaven had come to them with a measure of power; it had occupied a large area of their thought.

But there were wide spaces yet unsubdued to the obedience of the perfect law of liberty. The kingdom of heaven comes into every man's life very much as Israel came to Canaan: it enters in and intrenches itself. But there is still much land to be occupied; there are hostile tribes in many strongholds; there must be a great deal of active campaigning before the whole territory is subdued. The kingdom has come, but its sway must be confirmed and extended. It has not yet fully come. The prayer that our Lord taught us never loses its meaning. And therefore those disciples of John needed every day to hear the same injunction, — " Change your minds, for the kingdom of heaven is at hand." "You have gained some new conceptions of life and duty," — we can imagine the Baptist saying to them, — " by means of which the kingdom has drawn near to you, and taken possession of some portion of your life ; but there are many other changes which will need to be made from time to time, in your habitual thinking, in order that the kingdom may be more fully established in your life. You will need to change your minds about the King himself, to whom I have borne witness ; for your first thought of his kingdom will be altogether inadequate. When you get rid of your crude ideas about him, and perceive that the Messiah is not to be a temporal king, then the kingdom of God will have come nearer to you. Thus, year by year, you will be changing your minds; old thoughts about God and his Son and his Church and his Word will be passing away; new views, new meanings, new interpretations, will displace the old; you will constantly be renewed in the spirit of your minds. And thus, with these larger and more perfect conceptions of the truth as it is in Jesus, the kingdom of God will come to you with ever-increasing power; you will be able to apprehend with all saints what is the breadth and length and height and depth of the love of Christ, that you may be filled with the fullness of God."

All through those early days, the disciples were constantly getting new ideas, — revising their theories about Christ and his kingdom, throwing overboard their old notions and taking in a new stock of working theories. On that night, after the crucifixion, when the eleven, and those that were with them, heartsick and despairing, saw Jesus standing in the midst of them, and heard him saying, " Peace be unto you!"

a new conception entered into their minds, — a conception which revolutionized their lives. Another such new idea came with a shock on the day of Pentecost; another, in a different way, but no less effective, when the first council gathered in Jerusalem, and Paul and Barnabas showed the church how God had opened the door of faith unto the Gentiles. It was in a very imperfect and partial way that the kingdom of heaven came, at first, even to the twelve apostles. It was a good while before it got full possession of them; they had to change their minds over and over to make room for it. This fact appears in their writings.

" A comparison of the various types of New Testament doctrine shows us further that the Christian idea is there presented to us in various stages of development. The speeches of St. Peter recorded in the earlier chapters of the Acts of the Apostles represent a more primitive type than we see in the first Epistle ascribed to that apostle. The Epistle of St. James is elementary in its treatment of the Christian life and truth, while in St. Paul's Epistles we have a rich elaboration of the doctrine. St. Paul himself shows an advance from the comparative simplicity of what he wrote to the Thessalonians to the profound ideas of the Epistle to the Romans, and again a further advance, especially in Christology, in the Epistle to the Colossians. In St. John we not only have a choice and characteristic type of Christian doctrine: it is evident that we have also a later development. We are quite accustomed to this representation of progress in revelation; we see that it is in harmony with the divine method in nature: but still we may be slow to perceive what it involves. Different stages of progress, viewed side by side, necessarily present divergent aspects; sometimes they appear to be quite contradictory. Progress is not a smooth movement; it involves a struggle for existence and the survival of the fittest, — repudiation of the old, and painful assimilation of the new. The garment is rent; the wine-skin is burst." [1]

We are not concerned to deny that the progress through which these early disciples were passing was something other and deeper than a mere change of opinions. The Spirit of truth who had come to abide with them is also the Spirit of purity, of gentleness, of patience, of charity; they were all the while growing in grace, as well as in the knowledge of the truth. But the fact cannot be concealed that the intellectual changes through which they were passing were many and momentous: there never has been a time in the history of the church when the followers of Christ were changing their minds so rapidly and so radically as at this time. This is only saying that there never was another time when the mind of the church was so thoroughly alive.

There are many who seem to suppose that the approach of the kingdom of heaven in-

[1] *Faith and Criticism: Essays by Congregationalists,* pp. 70, 71.

duces a stationary mental condition among
men; or that if, upon this advent, any
change occurs in intellectual conceptions, it
is once for all; that the minds of those who
are brought under this sway become fixed in
a certain set of notions, and that it is a mark
of disloyalty if any sign of an inquiring disposition appears. That this would be contrary to all the analogies of nature is evident enough. Life, in every one of its
forms, produces constant changes: "Behold,
I make all things new," is its word of power.
And Paul seems to say that this law of
change is the law of the spiritual life: "If
any man be in Christ, he is a new creature;
the old things are passed away; behold, they
are become new." Though the outward man
may be decaying, he tells us, "the inward
man *is renewed day by day.*" What is the
inward man? Does the term designate only
the sentiments, the feelings? I suppose
that we have no right to put this narrow
construction upon it. The work of renewal
is intellectual as well as emotional. The

new hopes and loves spring from new thoughts, new aspects of life, new conceptions of duty. The attempt to keep one part of the inward man in bandages while the other parts are allowed to grow must result in deformity and feebleness. It would be easy to predict the result, even if we had not before our eyes so many illustrations of its fatal character.

It is evident, then, that new conceptions of Christian life and duty must always be in order. The substance of the Christian experience is permanent, but its forms are always changing ; its manifestations, like the grace from which they spring, are new every morning and fresh every evening. Loyalty to Christ, confidence in his word, readiness to know and do his will, — these are changeless principles of the Christian character ; but the question how I can best manifest this loyalty, by what message spoken, by what obedience rendered, is a question for every day. " New occasions teach new duties," and every new duty is the expression in concrete form of a new truth, — the embodiment in act of a new conception of life.

The truth must not be overlooked that, while the kingdom of heaven can only come to those who accept the new conceptions in which its meaning and power are conveyed, yet it is the presence of this kingdom which awakens these thoughts. The apparent contradiction is only the law of reciprocity which we encounter whenever we deal with the phenomena of life. It is the moisture of the earth that attracts the showers, and it is the showers that water the earth. Upon the desert no rain falls, and because no rain falls there it is a desert. Some things stand related to each other so reciprocally that each is both the cause and the effect of the other. The summer brings life to the tribes of earth, and the tribes of earth lead in the summer. The seed produces the plant and the plant produces the seed. What we have said, therefore, respecting new conceptions of truth as conditioning the progress of the kingdom does not conflict with the af-

firmation that it is the progress of the kingdom which gives rise to these new conceptions
of truth.   It was the growth of Christianity
which forced upon the council at Jerusalem
the truth that the Gentiles were fellow-heirs,
and the wider acceptance of that truth sped
the progress of Christianity.   It is the increase of Christian love — what Mr. Kidd
calls the accumulation of a great fund of
altruistic feeling — that has compelled the
adoption of a new philosophy of society, and
the adoption of that philosophy promotes
the growth of altruistic feeling.   The wholesome changes that have taken place in the
dogmas of the church have generally been
the response to a purified and heightened
ethical sentiment.   It was because the
kingdom of God was coming with increasing power that men were compelled to
change their minds about witchcraft, and
about the damnation of non-elect infants,
and about a good many other horrible doc-
trines.   And, conversely, the putting away
of these dreadful notions from their minds

has cleared the way for the coming of the kingdom of God.

The presence of the moral and spiritual forces by which the kingdom is revealed must, therefore, be signalized by many changes in men's conceptions of truth and duty. The larger life will call for ampler theories; the better practice will demand a better philosophy. It is the belief of the writer of these chapters that the kingdom of heaven is coming among men at this time with great power, and that therefore there is a loud call to men to change their minds. I am not denying, mark, that other changes than those of an intellectual nature are demanded; the need of a radical change in the ruling love and in the habitual conduct is not even questioned; but it is the object of this book to point out some of the changes in men's thinking which the present conditions of Christian society most clearly indicate. All of these changes are now in progress. Some minds have already passed through them. The new truth has been welcomed by these disciples, and the way of the kingdom into their lives has been prepared. No novelty will, therefore, be presented here. I shall only point out certain existing tendencies of thought which, as it seems to me, ought more and more to prevail, — certain ideas, already influential over many minds, which, when they are generally accepted, will greatly accelerate the progress of the kingdom.

II.

THE DOCTRINE OF FATHERHOOD.

Of the first man the scriptural idea is that he was created in the image of God: "So God created man in his own image, in the image of God created He him." This, if we connect with it the immediately following endowment of dominion over the earth, is the highest, the grandest, the most inspiring and ennobling idea and description of man ever given. There is in it essentially the idea of sonship, and so of the fatherhood of God. In its fullness this was first reached by Christ, but it was the scriptural idea from the beginning. Without the image there is no sonship. With it we have all that is implied in that, though the depth and fullness of the love of God as a Father could never have been apprehended except through Christ. — MARK HOPKINS, *The Scriptural Idea of Man*, page 1.

> Take all in a word : the truth in God's breast
> Sits trace for trace upon ours impressed ;
> Though He is so bright and we so dim,
> We are made in his image to witness Him.
>   ROBERT BROWNING, *Christmas Eve.*

Upon the race and upon the individual Jesus is always bringing into more and more perfect revelation the certain truth that man, and every man, is the child of God. This is the sum of the work of the Incarnation. A hundred other statements regarding it, regarding Him who was incarnate, are true ; but all statements concerning Him hold their truth within this truth, — that Jesus came to restore the fact of God's fatherhood to man's knowledge, and to its central place of power over man's life. — PHILLIPS BROOKS, *The Influence of Jesus*, page 12.

II.

THE DOCTRINE OF FATHERHOOD.

THE relation of man to God is a subject concerning which there is need of clearer ideas. The doctrine of the Divine Fatherhood has long been regarded as fundamental in theology; it lies so palpably upon the face of the New Testament that it could hardly be avoided; but the qualifications and limitations with which it has been held have greatly reduced its significance. Theoretically, God has been confessed to be the Father of men; but it has been assumed that, after all, it is only with the regenerate that any parental relations are maintained. The child, it seems to be supposed, has the power of annulling the fact of the fatherhood. This breach having been made, the real relation is no longer that of Father and child, but that of strangers and aliens; and

none of the benefits of the fatherhood are
within reach of the child until a change in
his status has somehow taken place. You
must tell men that God is their Father, but
you must be very careful not to let them
get the idea that they are his children.
The conception is difficult to entertain, but
there is force enough in it greatly to sophis-
ticate the ideas of men respecting the deepest fact of their lives.

Some of us who are fathers find it hard
to understand how a child can annul the
fact of fatherhood. It does not appear to
be a matter over which the will of the father
or the will of the child can have any control.
The relation is not contractual, and so termi-
nable by the choice of either party or of
both parties ; it is natural and unrepealable.
He who is bone of my bone and flesh of my
flesh cannot be other than my child, no matter what his wish or mine may be ; no matter what the laws may say ; no matter what
crimes he may commit, or by what enor-
mities he may outrage my fatherly feeling.

While he lives, and while I live, that relation will subsist. Nor can I understand how there could ever be any willingness on the part of a true father that the relation should be terminated. The obligations of fatherhood are not affected by the child's misconduct. The more disobedient and the more ungrateful he is, the stronger are the reasons why I should seek to save him. The time may come when I shall feel helpless to do anything for him; when my very love will forbid me to offer him relief and succor; when I shall see that the best medicine for him will be the fruit of his own doings: but there can never be a moment, in any world, when the heart of the father will not spring to help and save a child who is willing to be helped and saved. If we, being evil, cannot eradicate from our hearts parental instincts and obligations, how much less can the Father in heaven ignore or deny his fatherhood!

There need be no shrinking, then, from the clear affirmation that God is the Father of us all; and, having said this, we need not stultify ourselves by going on to deny that we are all his children. The distinction which theology has labored to make cannot be made by the human reason. The fact of the Divine Fatherhood, in all its fullness, with all its natural implications, must be distinctly declared. If it is true, it is the greatest truth of which any man can think, and we must not suffer it to be confused or belittled. To make every man see that, not according to some legal fiction, — not as the result of some possible pact or concession, — but according to the immediate and the everlasting fact, he is a child of God, made in the divine image, with all the possibilities and all the responsibilities of the sons of God resting now upon his conscience, is to bring the strongest possible motive to bear upon his life.

If he is living unworthily, if he is exposed to mortal peril, these facts need not be concealed, they may be all the more cogently asserted. The very misery and shame of his condition is this, that, being a child of God, he is where he is. The child cannot annul the fact of his paternity, but he can dishonor his Father and destroy himself. Fatherhood is not, alas! a barrier against ruin. The prodigal can spurn his Father's love and go into the far country, and can stay there, despite his Father's love, and perish there. But all the while he is his Father's child; it is the one truth that needs to be brought home to him : if anything can rouse him and reclaim him, it will be the recognition of this truth.

Another corollary of this truth is of vast moment. It means that goodness, the most glorious and perfect goodness, is, in the deepest sense of the word, natural to man. Evil may have become a second nature to him, but the evil impulses and tendencies are not his real self. " For the good which I would I do not, but the evil, which I would not, that I practice. But if what I would not, that I do, it is no more I that do it, but sin which dwelleth in me." The evil nature

is not I; it is a false, an artificial self, which
has usurped a power over me to which I
must not consent. I am a child of God,
and the divine impulses and motives which
I find in my heart are the real man. He
who comes to be the Revealer of God and the
Redeemer of man comes to help me to realize myself to be a man. In the words of a
great modern teacher: "There is no human
affection of fatherhood, brotherhood, child-
hood, which is not capable of expressing
divine relations. Man is a child of God,
for whom his Father's house is waiting.
The whole creation is groaning and travailing till man shall be complete. Christ
comes not to destroy but to fulfill. What
is the spirit of such words as these? Is it
not all a claiming of man through all his
life for God? Is it not an assertion that
just so far as he is not God's he is not
truly man? Is it not a declaration that
whatever he does in his true human nature,
undistorted, unperverted, is divinely done,
and therefore that the divine perfection of

his life will be in the direction which these
efforts of his nature indicate and pro-
phesy?"[1]

The clear apprehension of this truth, that
the work of redemption is just bringing
back man to his real self, would impart to
our gospel in many quarters a new significance. "He restoreth my soul." Is not
this, indeed, the very thing that he came to
do? Salvation came to the prodigal "when
he came to himself." Nothing better can
be done for the most degraded outcast than
to bring him to himself. Sin is temporary
insanity. The mind wanders. The man is
not himself. The restoration of clear thinking, the return of the power to comprehend
his own identity, this is the beginning of
the better life.

The notion that the Christian life is an
unnatural life; that in conversion we take
on a new and foreign selfhood; that the
sentiments and habits of the renewed man
are radically different from those of the

---

[1] *The Light of the World*, by Phillips Brooks, p. 7.

" natural " man, — all this grievously hinders the acceptance of our gospel, or perverts it, when it is accepted, into a caricature of itself.   Much of this is due to a crass and unspiritual exegesis, — to the hardening of Pauline metaphors into philosophical distinctions.   True, that Paul contrasts the natural man with the spiritual man; but what does he mean by " the natural man " ? True, that in many texts the hostility of the unregenerate nature to God is emphasized : but is it the real human nature that is thus characterized, or that artificial, second nature which has overgrown the true humanity; is it Paul's " I myself," or Paul's " the law in my members " ?   True, that " adoption " is spoken of as part of the work of salvation; but is this adoption a necessary legal process through which men must pass before they can become the children of God, or is it a rhetorical figure by which is signified the welcome of unfilial children returning to their loyalty ?   Can we really assume it to be a fact of theological science that

the filial relations of men to God have become so disturbed by sin that a legal process of restoration is necessary? What infinite confusion has been introduced into
our thinking about God by such attempts
to turn the language of feeling into the
language of science!

No; the real gospel truth is, that Christ
comes to put us in possession of ourselves, —
to help us to drive out the usurping powers
of darkness, and to take the rights and
dignities that belong to us as men. "Now
are we the sons of God," and He wants us
to know it and live up to it. "All of
our Christian thinking and talking," says
Bishop Brooks, "has been and is haunted
by a certain idea of failure and recommence-
ment. Man is a failure, so there shall be
a new attempt; and in place of the man we
will make the Christian! There is nothing
of that tone about what Jesus says. The
Christian to Jesus is the man. The Christian, to all who think the thought of Jesus
after Him, is the perfected and completed

man. Just see what this involves. Hear
with what naturalness it clothes the invita-
tions of the gospel. They are no strange
summons to some distant unseen land; they
are God's call to you to be yourself. They
appeal to a homesickness in your own heart,
and make it their confederate. That you
should be the thing you have been, and not
be that better thing, that new man which is
the oldest man, the first type and image of
your being, is unnatural and awful. . . . If
Christ can make you know yourself; if, as
you walk with Him day by day, He can re-
veal to you your sonship to the Father; if,
keeping daily company with Him, you can
more and more come to know how native is
goodness, and how unnatural sin is to the
soul of man; if, dwelling with Him who is
both God and man, you can come to believe
both in God and in man through Him, —
then you are saved, — saved from contempt,
saved from despair, saved into courage and
hope and charity, and the power to resist

temptation, and the passionate pursuit of perfectness." [1]

That this is a conception of the Christian life quite unlike that which has prevailed in most of our evangelical communions cannot, I think, be denied. That it is a distinctly higher and truer conception than those which have been current is scarcely debatable. The appeal which it makes to the human heart is far more inspiring; the possibilities which it sets before us more alluring. When this great truth gets full possession of the mind of the church, the kingdom of heaven will come with increasing power.

[1] *The Light of the World*, pp. 10, 22.

III.

THE DOCTRINE OF BROTHERHOOD.

Now there is another part of charity, which is the basis and pillar of this, and that is the love of God for whom we love our neighbor ; for this I think charity, to love God for himself, and our neighbor for God. All that is truly amiable is God, or, as it were, a divided piece of Him that retains a reflex or shadow of himself. Nor is it strange that we should place affection on that which is invisible ; all we truly love is thus. What we adore under affection of our senses deserves not the honor of so pure a title. Thus we adore Virtue, though to the eyes of sense she be invisible. Thus that part of our noble friends that we love is not the part which we embrace, but that invisible part which our arms cannot embrace. — SIR THOMAS BROWNE, *Religio Medici*, Part II., sect. xiv.

Giving is not a condescension. I must not assume that, because another man is poorer than I, I have a right to give him something. To fling him an alms may be an insult. A gift may serve to only degrade him. Let me look carefully at myself, at him, and at the gift before I dare bestow. Some of us have been too prone to think it quite proper that we should have most of the good things, and should bestow of our superfluity upon the rest of mankind, while they, duly feeling their dependence upon our bounty, are grateful. Perhaps, were the situation reversed, we should not be so ready to accept it. — MARY EMILY CASE, *The Love of the World*, page 81.

III.

THE DOCTRINE OF BROTHERHOOD.

THE coming of the kingdom of heaven will be signalized and hastened by the prevalence of clearer ideas respecting the brotherhood of man. When the doctrine of the Divine Fatherhood is rightly understood, the conceptions of men respecting their relations to one another must needs be clarified.

It is true, indeed, that the implications of this doctrine have already brought about mighty changes in the earth. The belief in the Divine Fatherhood has undermined feudalism and destroyed slavery and led in democracy. The power of this great idea it is, more than any or all other agencies, which has compelled the emancipation of the laboring classes, and the establishment, in so many nations, of political equality. If all

men are the sons of God, then it is plain
that one man may not enslave another, nor
oppress another, nor despise another. Some
measure of social fellowship must also follow as the inference from this doctrine. If
there are still differences among men, as
among the stars, and if some liberty of
social selection is allowed, so that those of
kindred tastes and aptitudes consort together,
— there is still no room left for the contempt
of the weaker and the more ignorant ; they
are all God's children, and respect and even
reverence must be due to every one of them.
" Honor all men. Love the brotherhood."
The haughtiness and exclusiveness which the
more fortunate sometimes exhibit towards
their lowlier brethren can never live in any
heart which has really comprehended the
truth of the Divine Fatherhood.

This doctrine of the equality of rights,
which springs from the Christian doctrine
of the Fatherhood of God, and which is the
corner-stone of our modern democracy, is
well established in the thought of the race.

The laws of great nations express it. The literature of the present century is saturated with it; it may be regarded as the ruling idea of modern civilization. The truth is not yet fully realized in our political and social life; vast injustices and inequalities are still arrayed against it; but it has taken possession of the mind of Christendom, and its ultimate victory over every form of social wrong is our reasonable expectation.

Not only with respect to political equality and social fraternity has the doctrine of human brotherhood found large realization, but also with respect to the practice of charity. The immense development of philanthropy which has characterized the Christian era is due to the partial realization of this truth. "'Any impartial observer,' says Mr. Lecky, 'would describe the most distinctive virtue referred to in the New Testament, as love, charity, or philanthropy.' It is the spirit of charity, pity, and infinite compassion which breathes through the gospel. The new religion was, at the outset, actually and without any figurative exaggeration, what the same writer has called it elsewhere, — a proclamation of the universal brotherhood of man.' We note how it was this feature which impressed the minds of men at first. The noble system of ethics; the affection which the members bore to each other; the devotion of all to the corporate welfare; the spirit of infinite tolerance for every weakness and inequality; the consequent tendency to the dissolution of social and class barriers of every kind, beginning with those between slave and master; and the presence everywhere of the feeling of actual brotherhood, — were the outward features of all the early Christian societies." [1]

This testimony indicates the close relation of Christianity not only to the development of charity, of which we are now speaking, but also to the development of social equality, of which we have just spoken. But while it is true that the brotherhood of man, as taught by Christ, has been largely

[1] *Social Evolution*, by Benjamin Kidd, p. 148.

the source of the abounding philanthropies
of the Christian era, it is also true that an
imperfect apprehension of this doctrine has
resulted in perverting charity, and in making the administration of it, in a vast number of cases, a curse rather than a blessing
to its recipients. Before the kingdom of
God can fully come, a great many Christian
people will have to change their minds concerning the true nature of charity.

Charity has been mainly almsgiving. The
assumption upon which it almost univer-
sally proceeds is the superiority of the giver
and the inferiority of the recipient. It is
a gracious act, originating in the benignity
of the bestower, and putting the beneficiary
under obligation. If the giver is not proud
and arrogant, he is at least complacent; if
the receiver is not humiliated, he is certainly
disposed to be very deferential. The act of
charity itself, as ordinarily conceived, puts
a difference between him who gives and him
who takes; it raises the one to a plane
somewhat above the other. It is probably

the truth to say that a great many of those who give are influenced to their bounty, in considerable degree, by the consciousness of superiority which is thus awakened. The tip, which is a kind of alms, is more willingly bestowed because it emphasizes the social contrast between the giver and the receiver. It is pleasant to have the power to confer favors, and to be able to make others realize this power. A good part of the blessedness of giving, in the heart of many a Lady Bountiful, may be traced to this source.

It is easy to see that the kind of brotherhood which is connoted by this subtle assumption of class distinctions is far removed from that true fraternity which springs from the clear recognition of every man as a child of God. When we have once comprehended the true character of the human beings whom we are trying to befriend, we cannot any longer indulge ourselves in such an undervaluation of them as is often signified in the looks and the words by which our alms are accompanied. If they, like ourselves, are God's dear children, they must be treated with respect and reverence, no matter how low they may have fallen. Our reverence and respect is the assertion of the truth which they are forgetting, and which they must by no means be permitted to forget. To treat them as though they were God's children is the only way to make some of them understand that they are his children. And if they are not degraded, if they are only unfortunate, then surely the air of superiority which the giver assumes is a palpable breach of the spirit of brotherhood.

The law of the brotherhood of man, as applied in our charities, requires, then, a genuine respect for the manhood and womanhood of all whom we are trying to help, — such a respect as will not for one moment consent to see them sink at our feet as menials, and kiss the hand of the benefactor; such a respect as will not permit them to cringe and fawn and flatter us, or willingly to assume the rôle of humble pensioners upon our bounty. Relations of this nature do not subsist between the children of a common Father. The fact that in all Christian communities a pauper class exists, and that in many of them it is steadily growing, is *prima facie* evidence that the true nature of the human brotherhood is not understood. Beyond all controversy, this pauper class owes its existence, in large measure, to the subtle selfishness of the almoners of charity, who are more willing to bestow a dole than to give a helping hand.

The fundamental error in all our charitable work is found, no doubt, in the conception that pain or suffering is the greatest of evils. This assumption is fundamental to much of our popular teaching, in the pulpit and out of it; and it is a false assumption. Suffering is not the greatest evil; moral unworthiness is the greatest evil. Suffering may often be disciplinary and remedial; falsehood, treachery, malignity, are evil and only evil. Between a willful choice of wrong and a severe infliction of pain, the pain is always to be chosen. It was not primarily from suffering or discomfort that Christ came to save men, but from sin and shame; from meanness and littleness; from the loss of the soul, which is the loss of character. The failure to comprehend this truth has resulted in the perversion and corruption of the Christian religion through centuries of history. Because men conceived that Christ's main purpose was to save men from suffering, all their administration of his gospel has been misdirected, and they have often aggravated the very evils which the gospel is intended to cure. In preaching the gospel chiefly as the means of escape from the sufferings of hell into the blessedness of heaven, the appeal was steadily made to the selfishness of men. And in the administration of charity, not less than in the methods of homiletics, the same error was committed. If Christ came to relieve men from suffering, that must be

the duty of all Christ's followers; and any
case of suffering must be relieved, no matter
at what cost to character. The question,
how the man is to be affected by this relief
of his immediate distress, is a question that
whole generations of Christians have forgot-
ten to ask.   Pain, they have assumed, is the
great evil: was it not from eternal pain
that Christ came to save us? and therefore
we must get this man out of pain, no matter
what happens to *him.*

Coupled with this was another false notion
which has had much to do with the perversion of charity. It has been supposed that
Christ's purpose to relieve suffering was so
central a part of his work of salvation that
he was willing to count any work of that
kind as special merit, and specially to reward
any one who gave relief to any sufferer; so
that he who mitigated any human woe by
that act laid up great treasure in heaven.
The bestowment of alms, therefore, upon any
one in poverty or distress was the crowning
Christian grace; it relieved suffering, which

was the chief purpose of Christ's mission, and it gained for the almsgiver a heavenly reward. Under the operation of these two motives, over large portions of the earth's surface, and for long periods, sweet charity has been turned into a curse. The mendicancy which has overrun Southern Europe is mainly due to this cause. All the hungry must be fed, all the naked must be clad, all beggars must receive alms, for this is the very substance of Christian virtue. What if the beggar be an impostor? You, at any rate, get the reward of your charity. If one is winning his way into heaven by his bounties, he must not trouble himself too much about their effect upon the recipients. Has not the Master said, " Give to him that asketh thee, and from him that would borrow of thee turn not thou away "? Why should we be scrupulous? Is not charity a good thing in itself? Out of such reasonings has sprung the beggary of Italy, of France, of Spain, of Ireland. The Spanish beggars get the point, and put it sharply in their habitual supplication, "Be good to your-self!" They will not allow you to forget that your almsgiving is in large measure a scheme to benefit yourself.

Notions similar to these vitiate a great deal of our own thought about charity. If there is not so much reference among us to the gains which we hope to get from our alms, there is constant assumption that the relief of suffering and want is always meri-torious; that the Christian must, because he is a Christian, relieve every case of suffer-ing and want that comes within his notice, immediately and without regard to any ul-terior consequences; that the refusal to do this in any case proves the man to be a hypocrite; that charity is such a good thing that there cannot possibly be too much of it; that the best Christian is the man who gives most and asks no questions; that what happens to those who receive what is given is a matter of small consequence.

Over against all this it is necessary to keep steadily before us the fact that Christ did not come into this world to relieve suffering. That was not the primary purpose for which he came. He came to save men from sin. Suffering is no doubt the consequence of sin, one of its consequences, — by no means its worst consequence; but Christ attacks the cause rather than the consequences. That he did relieve much suffering is true; but we must not fail to see how wholly subordinate was this work of physical relief to the work of restoring character, of redeeming men from the power of sin. Always he insisted that this ministry to the bodies of men was but the sign and illustration of the greater work which he had come to do for their souls. To care for bodily needs, and ignore the effect of what we are doing upon the manhood of the recipient, is a curious way of imitating Christ.

Now, if Christ did not come primarily to relieve suffering, then it is not the Christian's first business to relieve suffering. Suffering is not the greatest evil. Suffering is a consequence, and not a cause; and we often make a great mistake in trying to remove the consequence without touching the cause, — leaving the cause, indeed, actively at work to produce more suffering. Much of our work of relief is at best only the lotion that soothes the eruption on the skin, while the poison in the blood is left to do its deadly work; often, alas! it is a lotion that adds to the virulence of the poison. The relief is momentary, the malady is aggravated. We must learn that suffering is not, under all circumstances, an evil. It may be natural, remedial, wholesome in its effects. Its connection with misdoing or non-doing may be close and salutary; and it may be of the very first importance that the sufferer should see this connection, and should be convinced that it is natural and inevitable. I see a great deal of suffering which I would not lift my finger to remove. I do not think that it would be right for me to do so. The one thing, above all others, which these sufferers must learn, is the connection between their suffering and their

own misdoing. The suffering is the good
ordinance of a good God, and this is the
fact which they need to know. For me to
step in and prevent them from learning it
would not be a good service to them. People sometimes say to me, "How can there
be a good God? If there were a good God
I should not suffer so." One cannot always tell such people the truth. One must
not, indeed, undertake to pronounce God's
judgments. But it seems, not seldom, to
one who looks on with human discernment,
that there would be very little evidence of
the existence of a good God if some of
these people did not suffer; that a merciful
Being could not let them go on destroying
themselves without some sharp reminders
of the danger into which they are so will-
fully plunging. I do not deny that there
are sufferings in this world, many and dire
sufferings, which no human discernment can
explain; which we cannot, by our sharpest
insight, connect with any known misdoing
of the sufferers. I do not pretend to say

that there are no mysteries connected with suffering, nor that the faith of men may not be sorely tried by the discipline through which they are called to pass. I only say that in many cases the relation of the suffering to the misdoing of which it is the consequence is clear and palpable; that its beneficent uses may be clearly seen; that it can be relieved by the sufferer himself if he will cease from his misdoing; that the removal of his suffering by others, who thus permit and encourage him to go on with his misdoing, is a clear interference with the natural order, which in this case is working remedially and beneficently.

These closely related misconceptions — first, that the relief of suffering is the deepest and most imperative need of human beings, and, second, that we find in the alleviation of the sufferings of our fellow-men our greatest opportunity to win the applause of . Heaven, and to secure for ourselves a high place among the saints — have strongly tended to the perversion of our charities.

I must not be understood as denying that much wise and benign work has been done in the name of charity; I am only saying that with the good a vast amount of evil has been mingled, and I am trying to point out the sources of the evil. And you will always find that practical failures of this kind spring from false or defective ideas. What these defective ideas are, in the case before us, we have seen. And it is plain that they must at once be cleared away by a distinct recognition of the great fact of human brotherhood.

If the mendicant — or the man who is sinking toward mendicancy — is my brother, child of the same Father, partaker of the same divine nature, heir of the same birthright, character in him is just as precious as it is in me; and I must choose for him, as I would for myself, manhood before comfort, freedom from shame and dishonor rather than relief from pain. If he is sinking below the level of manhood, that degradation ought to be attended with suffering; the suffering is the divine admonition to arouse himself, and resist the downward tendencies. I must not silence that voice, I must call his attention to its significance; and my first duty is to take him by the hand and help him to reascend to the safer levels from which he has been sinking. If I find a fellow-man in a quagmire, my duty is not to try to make him comfortable there, but to get him out.

The man who asks an alms is a free spirit, inhabiting a body of flesh. The material part is deserving of care and honor, but only because it is, for a few years, the tabernacle inhabited by the spiritual part. The body is the handiwork of God, the spirit is his offspring. Surely it is the spiritual rather than the physical part of man which is made in the divine image. When we say that God is the Father of us all, we mean that he is the Father of our spirits; and therefore the brotherhood of man is chiefly a spiritual fact, and the law of that brotherhood is chiefly concerned with spiritual interests. We manifest our brotherhood most clearly by keeping uppermost the great facts of character. When, therefore, my neighbor asks an alms, my question must be, not merely what must be the effect of the bestowal of the alms upon his physical comfort, but also and chiefly how it will affect his spiritual condition. Will it make him more or less a man if I encourage him in living upon alms? I have compassion for his bodily distresses, but should not my deepest and keenest sympathy take hold upon that part of his nature in which our kinship is closest? How can I bear to see him sinking into an unmanly dependence?

We cannot be unmindful of bodily suffering; we shall do what we can to relieve it, when anything can be done without entailing spiritual losses; but we shall be far more profoundly affected by everything which threatens to impair the spiritual integrity of our brother. It is the injuries and losses with which the man himself is threatened that most appeal to our sympathy, — not the damage that may be done to the house he lives in.

The conception of our relation to our brother as one which encourages us to utilize his misfortunes for our own profit is even more abhorrent. The indulgence of humane and compassionate feelings is, no doubt, a luxury to some natures. And there are those who suppose that the indulgence of such feelings makes up the greater part of human virtue. The poor and the suffering are mainly interesting to some persons because they furnish an occasion for the indulgence of these feelings. We have the poor and the suffering always with us, and we are therefore always supplied with an incentive to acts by which we may gratify our sensibilities, and at the same time greatly advance our own interests. They are simply objects on which we may practice our compassions. It is in such practice that we develop the saintly virtues, and gain high seats in heaven. What may become of them is not the first concern with us; we are looking out for our own salvation.

I am depicting this state of mind with rather a blunt pencil; probably very few persons have ever stated the case to themselves in terms quite so bald and repulsive ; but the tendency will be recognized. And it is not difficult to see that such a tendency is the explicit contradiction of the fact of brotherhood. The man who flings a dole to a beggar, not knowing nor caring how much it debases him, only hoping to be sped thereby in his own path to heaven, is one who has never thought of this beggar as his brother.

But has not Christ himself said, " It is more blessed to give than to receive "? Truly he has; and, in the words of Dr. Bascom, " the failure to take the highest social principle from the lips of Christ is seen in the very partial way in which it is applied when men first turn to it. They may give, but give with so little wisdom

and love, — give in such antagonism to
lower principles, — as quite to lose sight
of the idea that giving is for the development of power.   A love that seeks virtuous
life will be saved from this error.   Giving
which is careless giving is not true giving,
as it lacks the giving mind and heart, and
cannot bear, either backward or forward,
to giver or receiver, the beneficence of a
gift.   The giving which is more blessed
than receiving is that which pours life into
channels of life, and draws life freshly there-
from." [1]

This, then, is the test of our charity, —
does it recognize between giver and receiver
the highest bond, the bond of spiritual brotherhood; and does it seek to make the gift
a vehicle for the communication of the divine life from the one to the other?   The
charity that does this is twice blessed.   The
charity that stuffs the cupboard and lets
the character starve; the charity that pros-
trates the receiver before the giver, and

[1] *Words of Christ*, p. 158.

makes the one a stepping-stone on which the other mounts to beatitude, — is twice cursed: it curseth him that gives and him that takes.

If those who ask for charity are our brethren, we must not wantonly or carelessly contribute to their degradation. We must love them as we love ourselves. We must hate the spirit of abjectness and servility and indolent mendicancy in them as we hate it in ourselves. What we know to be beneath the dignity of the sons of God in us is not to be tolerated in them. For them to be beggars and sponges is a sorrow and a disgrace to us, for they are the children of our Father. By some means they must be rescued from this fate. We must save them. If brotherhood means anything at all, it can mean no less than this.

"There is," says a modern preacher, " I am thankful to believe, much kindness in the hearts of very many toward their poorer brethren; there is abundant discussion of the methods by which they are to be helped. But there is not nearly as much kindness as there ought to be in the hearts of professing Christians: how can there be until each one of us is filled with the mind of Him who came down from heaven to suffer and die for his brethren? The true compassion is that which longs to make each brother better, happier, safer, as a child of God; no compassion which stops short at the temporal condition of the poor is worthy of them or of us, or will be effectual in reaching even its own ends. The pity, the goodwill, which deserves to be called Christian love, will be powerful enough to engage all the energies of the mind, all the resources of experience, in the service of the poor. Making us more interested, more careful, more anxious in that service, it would also restlessly impel us to give, not less but more. The true Christian will not dare to call anything that he has his own: he will go beyond Mr. Henry George or Mr. Hyndman in confessing the claims of the great suffering mass of humanity, not only upon all that he possesses, but upon himself; he

will count himself as sent into the world
to administer whatever is intrusted to him
to the glory of God, and therefore to the
advantage of his fellows." [1]

It will be evident, from these reflections,
that the business of charity is a high and
sacred vocation. No man can rightly administer it who does not first clearly understand and deeply feel the dignity and di-
vineness of human nature. No man can
bestow charity worthily who does not know
that he himself is a child of God, and who
does not feel a deep sense of the sacredness
of that relation. Unless he has, consciously
or unconsciously, fellowship with the Father ;
unless God's purposes for man are the ruling of his life, — he has nothing really valu-
able to give to those in need.

And it is equally needful that he should
comprehend with equal clearness the truth
that every beggar at his door is as truly
God's child as he is, and that God's purposes
concerning this beggar brother must be the

[1] *Social Questions :* by J. Llewellyn Davies, p. 286.

guide of all his conduct toward him. The
kind of ministry that the beggar has a right
to receive from him is that which will enable him to realize his manhood. Christ
has come to help every man to recover the
manhood he has lost, to realize the purpose for which he was created. He is the
Elder Brother, the Captain of Salvation;
and we follow Him in the work of forgiving
and saving men. We know how He saved
them: He lived among them; He lived for
them; He gave his life in an untiring ministry to them. He did relieve their physical sufferings, but never without seeking to
restore their lost manhood. To bring them
all back to the Father, to make them see
what manner of love He has bestowed upon
them, and what manner of men they ought
to be because they were children of such a
Father, — this was the whole purpose of his
ministry. In Him was life, and the life
was the light of men.

" Still," says Dr. Hodges (and he is talking about the lad whom Jesus healed at the

foot of the Mount of Transfiguration), " it is significant that not only here but elsewhere Jesus got very close to the man whom he would help. It means something that He took him by the hand. He was forever doing that. Throughout his ministry He dealt with individuals, not with crowds. He went among the people, never holding himself aloof from them ; coming into personal acquaintance with their temptations, bearing their sicknesses, and carrying their sorrows. He was called the friend of publicans and sinners. And the name was a true description of his ministry among them. He talked with them, walked with them, ate at their tables, knew the names of their little children ; He helped them, not so much by what He said as by what He was. He won their hearts and changed their lives, not by his sermons, but by his blessed friendship. He took them by the hand ; thus he lifted them up and they arose." [1]

He was the Elder Brother. His life is

---

[1] *The Heresy of Cain,* p. 24.

the perfect manifestation of the divine human brotherhood. His way of doing good is the true method of charity.

We are trying, in these latter days, to learn this method. We call it sometimes the new charity. To minds sophisticated by the old notions of almsgiving it seems, indeed, a revelation; and it is doubtful whether, in any age, the church of Christ has grasped the full meaning of this fact of brotherhood as related to the work of charity. To the multitude it is a new conception, — one of those which is, we trust, to revolutionize our philanthropic enterprises. But there must have been, in a day long past, in Galilee and Decapolis and Jerusalem and beyond Jordan, many who saw this brotherhood revealed in its most perfect pattern.

IV.

THE ONE AND THE MANY.

Our theory of individualism — of each one for himself within the limits of the law, and those limits not too tightly drawn — must be qualified. The knowledge of the solidarity of interests, that all workers live by and through each other's labor, whether of hand or head, and that we all live by and through the accumulated results of science and civilization, should teach us that the benefits and blessings of civilization should not be monopolized by any class, that morally they belong to all. Our theory of private property will require revision and limitation. While in its essence the principle of private property must continue, — being, as we have seen, both an instinct of our nature, generated and continually intensified by twenty centuries of existence under it, as well as a necessity of our complicated and ever-expanding modern life, — nevertheless there must be a new conception of it, of the rights which it is supposed to imply, and very particularly of the obligations which it should impose on its possessor. The latter will have to be increased and emphasized; the former will have to be curtailed. — WILLIAM GRAHAM, *The Labor Problem*, page 347.

The unity that comes through organization is not so easy to define. It transcends space, almost annihilates time, defies mathematics, and is the despair of formal logic. The whole is in the parts, the parts are in the whole. There is an instantaneous response of each member to the condition of every other. The whole is more than the sum of its parts, and the internal relationships are so subtle that they cannot be adequately expressed in terms of action and reaction from without. The secret of this organic life is the nervous system, which binds each part to every other, makes the whole responsive to the needs of every part, and every part an instrument for the futherance of the needs of the whole. The whole gives to the parts whatever meaning and significance they have, and the parts in turn give to the whole whatever expression and realization it attains. — WILLIAM DE WITT HYDE, *Outlines of Social Theology*, page 247.

THE ONE AND THE MANY.

In the New Testament teaching about conduct two truths are emphasized, — the independence of the individual, the solidarity of society.

In many passages the nature of moral responsibility as personal and individual is clearly affirmed. The fact that guilt and blameworthiness are not transferable; that every man must bear his own burden; that every man must give account of himself unto God; that every man must work out his own salvation; that the converting grace always awaits the choice of the individual, — all this is made very plain. The evangelistic teaching of later years has wrought out this truth in high relief. It was a truth that needed emphasis, because it had been somewhat obscured by the Augustinian theology;

but the emphasis has been greatly exaggerated. The solitariness of religious experience must not be denied, but neither must it be unduly magnified. Out of it may easily grow an unholy egoism which is far from the spirit of Christ.

When the penitent is exhorted to believe that Christ died for him; that the question of salvation is a purely personal matter between himself and his Saviour: that he must put all other suppliants out of his mind, and think of himself as standing solitary before the bar of judgment or the throne of grace, — we know what the exhortation means, and perceive the deep truth that underlies it; but it is quite possible that the words may convey a wrong impression of the isolation of man in the act of salvation.

The autobiographies of saints once regarded as eminent, with their minute records of all the varying shades of individual experience, marking them now as the subjects of special divine displeasure, and now as the favorites of Heaven, represent a kind of pious egotism which is shocking to all right feeling. In large sections of the Christian church, the crucial question respecting the Christian life is, " How do you feel? " Salvation, or at any rate the evidence of it, is, according to this view, a satisfied and pleasurable feeling. Now, feeling is a purely personal matter ; and the religious experience in which it is made the test must be of a very individualistic type. The religiousness which rests upon this foundation may easily coexist with a high degree of selfishness. When one learns in his devotions that his own personal satisfaction is the main concern, it will not be strange if he acts on that principle in other affairs. And those who make the most of their own personal moods and tenses in the matter of religion are the kind of persons who can easily convince themselves that they could be happy in heaven while their next of kin were weltering in everlasting torment.

The religious experience which springs

from such an exaggerated idea of the independence of the individual is likely to
bear fruit in the social world. It easily
falls in with that atomistic theory of society
in which individual rights count for everything, and social obligations for little or
nothing. The methods which it finds ready
to its hand are those of unrestricted competition; its motto is, "Every man for himself." That there is to be a certain measure of unity and coöperation in society is,
of course, allowed; but this is not to be consciously sought: it is to be brought about
by an overruling Providence, under the
sway of those economic harmonies whose
function it is to resolve selfish intentions
into benevolent issues. We are slowly
finding out that this is a misplaced confidence; that when the individuals of which
society is composed are all as selfish as they
can be, the millennium rather tardily ar-
rives. And it is already evident that a
social philosophy whose principle is pure
individualism can never give us the formula

of a peaceful and prosperous society. The exaggeration of this doctrine of the independence of the individual bears no better fruit in sociology than in morals or religion.

The other doctrine of the solidarity of society has been subject also to much disproportionate statement. No doctrine is more clearly taught in the New Testament; the truth that " we are members one of another " lies at the foundation of much of Paul's reasoning. The Adamic headship, also, whatever theological interpretation be given to it, involves the organic character of the human race and the tremendous facts of heredity. " Through one man sin entered into the world, and death through sin ; and so death passed unto all men, for that all sinned." " For as through the one man's disobedience the many were made sinners, even so through the obedience of the one shall the many be made righteous." " For as in Adam all die, even so in Christ shall all be made alive." Doubtless it is a great abuse to harden these glowing words

into logical statements; none the less they
do convey to every reader some sense of
an organic unity of mankind by which the
stock conceptions of theological individualism must be greatly modified.   How much
use has been made of these statements of
human solidarity, I do not need to say.
They have dominated the theology of large
sections of the church, to the practical sup-
pression of the truth of responsibility.   And
this doctrine, too, or something closely akin
to it, has found its way into sociology.   Theories which represent the individual as having very little distinct character, as being
the product of the social conditions under
which he lives, have had numerous de-
fenders, and there is a great truth here
which no man can deny.   " Each nation
and tribe," says one writer, " produces in
its children its own type of character, which
has grown up in it, through the influence of
the physical surroundings and past history
of the people.   Each individual is not a
new phenomenon in the world, but only one

particular specimen of a race, whether he be
'a yeoman whose limbs were made in Eng-
land,' a painter whose eyes were developed
in Italy, or a philosopher whose brain grew
in Germany. And after the individual has
been produced, with his particular type of
potential character, the direction in which
that character develops is determined by
the habits and customs of his particular
people and class. . . . From this point of
view there is an obvious sense in which the
relation of the individual to his society is
an intrinsic one. His life is controlled
both by the dead and by the living, among
his people. He is what his fathers have
been before him, except in so far as he has
breathed a different air. Nor is this influence of social environment something purely
external, by which the individual is affected.
There is not first the individual, and then
the influences which mould his life. He is
nothing except what he has become through
the influence of that spiritual setting. There
is nothing deeper in our nature than our

inherited traits; there is nothing more our own than our natural disposition and sentiments; there is nothing by which we are more possessed than the spirit of our time. We cannot go behind the elements of our constitution to find something deeper which we can regard as our very self, and which is prior to such impressions. They are the elements out of which our self has grown, and we can find nothing beyond them that in any deeper sense belongs to us, or that in any deeper sense is *we*." [1]

All this shows how closely our intellectual lives are linked with the life of the generation in which we live, of the race from which we spring. Yet this doctrine of solidarity, like the doctrine of individualism, is often overstated. That man is identified with his kind is profoundly true; but it is not true that in his fraternity he loses his identity. He cannot realize his own life apart from society, yet his relation

---

[1] *An Introduction to Social Philosophy*, by J. S. Mackenzie, p. 150.

to society is not that of the Brahman to his deity. There is a social philosophy which dissolves the individual; society is conceived as the menstruum in which the individual disappears. The exaggeration of solidarity, which underlies some theories of socialism, is quite as common as the exaggeration of individualism, and no less misleading.

The error of individualism may be illustrated by comparing society to a heap of sand. The individuals of which society is composed are like the separate grains of sand. They are entirely independent of each other; none of them is affected in any way by any of the rest; there is no giving or receiving among them; there is not even any cohesion; there is simply aggregation. None of these grains of sand is any more or less a grain of sand because it happens to lie in this heap; it would have precisely the same constitution and the same powers and properties if it were all alone by itself anywhere in the universe.

Now, the view of the extreme individualist tends toward a representation of society as somewhat resembling a sand-heap. Nobody would adopt any such illustration, but much of the reasoning of many individualists suggests a kind of isolation and independence which is something like this. " A monadistic view of society," says Professor Mackenzie, " would be one which regarded all the individuals of whom the society is composed as by nature independent of each other, and as connected together only by a kind of accidental juxtaposition. Such a view would naturally lead to the conclusion that the connection of individuals in a society tends to interfere with the natural development of the individual life, and that it would be better for the individuals if they could manage to live apart." [1]

In truth, the theory of the social contracts, upon which much of the political philosophy of recent times has been based, is often interpreted as meaning that the indi-

[1] *Introduction to Social Philosophy*, p. 135.

vidual, in entering society, actually divests himself of a portion of his personal rights, — reduces, to a considerable extent, the sum of his powers. The noble savage in the state of nature is, according to this view, a completer man than the member of a civilized community. All those who think, with Mr. Herbert Spencer, that government is a necessary evil, rest their belief upon this assumption. And those who go a little further than Mr. Spencer, and preach that government is an unnecessary evil — that it is wholly accursed and injurious — carry the theory of individualism to its logical issue. A thoroughly consistent individualist is, of course, an anarchist. The absolute independence of the individual is the negation of social order and of political society. Mr. Spencer, in the earlier editions of his "Social Statics," enumerates among the fundamental rights of man " the right to ignore the state," " the right of the citizen to adopt a condition of voluntary outlawry. If every man," he says, " has freedom to do

all that he wills, provided he infringes not
the equal freedom of any other man, then
he is free to drop connection with the state,
— to relinquish its protection and to refuse
paying toward its support." I do not think
that Mr. Spencer would wish to be held
responsible to-day for this language, but it
is a fair statement of the logical outcome of
a doctrine which makes the individual everything and the social order nothing.

The error of socialism, on the other hand,
may be illustrated by comparing society to
a chemical compound, into which the various ingredients enter by surrendering their
own proper constitution, and becoming un-
distinguishable elements in the new substance. "In a chemical combination," says
Professor Mackenzie, "the parts are not intrinsically related to the whole, but are rather
lost in the whole. So long as they continue
to exist as separate parts they are independent of the whole, but in the whole they
become transfigured. Nor can there be
any development in such a system, nor any

end towards which a development could be directed : the parts are swallowed up in the whole, so that nothing further can take place in the system except by its dissolution." [1]   This is the logical basis of the philosophy of socialism ; and its outcome would be a view of society "which regarded the union of human beings as the primary fact with regard to them, and the individual life as the mere outcome of social conditions. The natural conclusion of this view would be that the individual has no right to any independent life of his own ; that he owes all that he is and has to the society in which he is born; and that society may fairly use him as a mere means to its development." [2]

The chemical illustration doubtless overstates the error of the socialists as much as the illustration of the sand-heap overstates the error of the individualists ; but, like that other illustration, it shows us the direction

---

[1] *Introduction to Social Philosophy*, p. 147.

[2] *Ibid.*, p. 135.

in which the theory is traveling. And it must be owned that, with many socialistic philosophers, it has traveled far in this direction. The socialistic contention certainly does lay so much stress on the improvement of the mass that it ignores or greatly undervalues the integrity of the individual. This is its inherent weakness. The most acute of modern critics has solid ground under his feet when he declares that the socialist polemic against private property "betrays an entire blindness to the essential elements of the social organism, which can only exist as a structure of free individual wills, each entertaining the social purpose in an individual form appropriate to its structural position and organic functions." [1]

We can make this clear by considering that property, private property, is the condition of the best social order. The best social order results from the social union and co-

---

[1] *The Civilization of Christianity*, by Bernard Bosanquet, p. 329.

operation of the highest type of men and women; and the highest type of manhood and womanhood can only be produced when men and women have the free use of property. Property is, indeed, the raw material for the development of character. It is in property, Hegel says, that my will is made real for me as a personal will. Property is the concentrated form of power, and it is in the exercise of power that my will is trained and disciplined.

It is in the realm of property rights and obligations that my personality is largely shaped. Until I have learned to use property conscientiously and beneficently, I have not equipped myself for the highest service of my fellow-men. In making it the instrument of promoting human welfare, more than in any other possible way, I socialize my own will, and prepare myself to enter into helpful relations with my fellow-men. I cannot learn this lesson in the use of property which I hold in common with my fellows. It must be my own; I must be free to express my own will in dealing with it; I cannot be unselfish in the use of that which is not mine; the most direct and effective discipline in unselfishness is that which is gained in using private property beneficently.

The fundamental assumption of socialism seems to be that if men possess private property they will use it selfishly; therefore, the socialists say, we will have no private property. The remedy would not be effectual. It is rather difficult to abolish all vestiges of private property. Hands and feet and eyes and tongues are possessions and instruments not easily alienated, and those who would use money or machinery selfishly would be quite sure to go on using all their personal powers in the same way after they were divested of money and machinery; claws and fists and elbows and teeth would still be private property, and a very unsocial use might be made of them. Unless the will has been socialized, unless men have learned how to use all their powers and possessions for the common welfare, the society in which they live will bear very little resemblance to heaven, no matter how small their personal belongings may be.

We are told, indeed, by modern expositors of socialism, that their scheme does not contemplate the abolition of private property in income, but only of private property in the means of production. All incomes would be the remuneration of labor, and would be paid by the state in labor checks entitling the receiver to specified amounts of goods in the public stores. The receiver might expend them as he pleased ; he might also give them away, or hoard them : he could not openly lend them upon interest, for the law would forbid that ; nor could he employ them in any kind of profitable traffic. In a certain limited sense, therefore, the recent socialists provide for private property. And a certain narrow discipline would be gained by frugality, conscientiousness, and benevolence in the use of this

private income. But all that larger discipline to which I have referred, which comes
through the socialization of the will by the
beneficent use of property in productive
enterprises, — in making it the servant of
a broad-minded philanthropy, — would be
impossible under socialism. And it seems
to me that the prohibition of private enterprise — of the productive use of property as capital, of the free exercise by
individuals of the power which property
confers — would greatly limit the range
of human development. It is true that it
would remove many temptations, and that
it would take from cruel hands a great instrument of oppression ; but is it not, after
all, better to let men have power and teach
them how to use it? It must be remembered that the socialistic programme rests
upon a profound disbelief in the possibility
of socializing the individual will, and in this
I find its condemnation.

A society composed of persons who were
the possessors of goods which they called

their own, but which they had learned to
use freely in the promotion of the common
welfare, would be a good society; while a
society based upon the assumption that all
that a man has will be used selfishly, and
that therefore the range of individual possession must be sharply limited, is perfectly
certain to be a very bad society.

The chemical solution of individual rights
which the socialists propose is likely to form
a highly explosive mixture.

Neither the sand-heap nor the chemical
compound furnishes us a good analogy of
the structure of human society. Is it possible for us to find a better analogy? I
believe that it is, and that we shall find
our most helpful suggestion in that figure
of the living organism which Paul, in one
form or another, so frequently uses. Doubtless the biological analogies all fail at certain points; our parables will not go upon
all-fours; and there are certain important
respects in which the social organism differs
essentially from that of the plant or the ani-

mal. But this illustration takes us nearer to the truth than any other which the kingdoms of nature furnish us. Paul gives us the thought in that passage of his in the Ephesians in which he speaks of the work of the Holy Spirit in the world as the building up of " the body of Christ." By " speaking truth in love," he says, " we may grow up in all things unto Him which is the head, even Christ; from whom the whole body, fitly framed and knit together through that which every joint supplieth, according to the working in due measure of each several part, maketh the increase of the body unto the building up of itself in love." Here is the true account of the relation of the one to the many. In the highest sense the many are one, — one body: but the union is not chemical, it is organic; the parts have an identity of their own; each one of the many is one, but it finds its life in the life of the larger unity. It is through that service which every organ supplieth that the organism lives; it is by the working in due measure of each several part that the body grows; and yet it is one body, and none of the members has any life or meaning or value in itself apart from the body. The relation of the members to the body is very different from the relation of the grains of sand to the sand-heap on the one hand, and from the relation of the several ingredients of the chemical compound on the other: there is a real unity, as there is not in the sand-heap; and there is the harmony of separate parts and powers, as there is not in the chemical solution which destroys the identity of the substances composing it. "An organism," says Professor Mackenzie, "is a real whole in a sense in which no other kind of unity is so. It is *in scipso totus, teres, atque rotundus.*" All its parts belong to it; they cannot be altered, so to speak, without its own consent; and the end which it seeks is also its own. At the same time it is a universe and not a unit; it has parts; and it does grow, and it has an end. We may define it, therefore, as a whole whose parts are intrinsically related to it, which develops from within, and has reference to an end that is involved in its own nature." [1]

We have had a good deal of discussion, some of it not over-clear, upon this question of the organic nature of human society. But Mr. Mackenzie's generalization which I have just quoted does, I believe, accurately describe human society. It is "a whole whose parts are intrinsically related to it." The individual cannot be separated from the society in which he lives and retain his individuality. The "organic filaments" which bind him to his fellow-men are vital elements in his own life, and they are constantly multiplying. "Thus," says Mr. Bosanquet, " if the individual in ancient Greece was like a centre to which a thousand threads of relation were attached, the individual in modern Europe might be compared to a centre on which there hang many, many millions." So far is it from being

[1] *Introduction to Social Philosophy*, p. 148.

true that society is constituted by the voli-
tional action of persons, that it is even true
that the "person," as we know him to-day,
is the product of social development. "The
unit of an ancient society was the family, of
a modern society the individual." So says
Sir Henry Maine. "Persons," with definite
rights, are the fruit of social progress.
This is not to say that the conscious moral
force of the individual himself has not
helped towards this emancipation, but he
never could have won it except through the
medium of society. "The individual *person*," says Mr. Ritchie, "the citizen with
rights and duties, is a complex of ideas, emotions, and aspirations which are altogether
unintelligible except as the product of cease-
less action and reaction in the spiritual
(*i. e.* intellectual, moral, etc.) environment,
which not merely surrounds, but actually
constitutes, the individual, — *i. e.* makes him
what he is. The history of the individual
cannot be understood apart from the history of the race, though of course in prac-

tice we have to limit ourselves to a small portion." [1]

This vital relation of the individual to the society of which he is a member is the one fruitful thought of modern times. It is easy to run it into absurdity by trying to find in society parts or organs analogous to every part or organ of the human body; nevertheless the conception is extremely fruitful, and, as a help in escaping from the barren immoralities of the old individualism, we cannot be too thankful for it. It is important to mark the differences between the social organism and the biological structures to which it is assimilated. "The truth is," says Mr. Ritchie, "that society (or the state) is not an organism because we can compare it to a beast or a man, but because it cannot be understood by the help of any lower — *i. e.* less complex — conception than that of organism. In it, as in an organism, every part is conditioned by the whole. In a mere aggregate or heap, the

[1] *Principles of State Interference*, p. 15.

units are prior to the whole; in an organism, the whole is prior to the parts, — *i. e.* they can only be understood in reference to the whole. But because the conception of an organism is more adequate to society than the conception of an artificial compound, it does not follow that it is fully adequate." [1]

Social organisms, as the same writer suggests, differ from other organisms in having the remarkable property of making themselves. There is a dynamic of the spirit here, for which no analogy can be found in the biological structures. And in truth it appears, as I have already hinted, that the very progress of society is toward the development of individuality, and society becomes more and more thoroughly organized through the consentaneous action of individual wills. " If it is true," says Mr. Mackenzie, " that the individual is formed by the habits and customs of his people, it is true also that the habits and customs of

[1] *Principles of State Interference*, p. 49.

the people grow out of the characters of the individual citizen. The relation of the individual to society is similar in kind to the relation of the will of an individual to his character. As will is the expression of character, so is the individual the expression of his society; but as change of character takes place only through acts of will, so a change in society takes place only through change in its individual members. And just as our wills are free, although they are the expression of our characters, so the individual has an independent life, although he is the expression of his society." [1]

This admirable statement will enable us to hold fast to the two contrasted truths in whose coördination we find the law of society. Such an organism as is here clearly indicated, society certainly is; and the power to recognize these subtle relations, and to adapt our voluntary efforts at construction to the facts of the case, should be sought by all social reformers.

[1] *Introduction to Social Philosophy,* p. 157.

It may be supposed that a discussion like this of the theory of society, of the relation of the one to the many, is of no practical value. "It is interesting," it may be said; "it satisfies our intellectual cravings, but has nothing to do with every-day life." On the contrary, I believe that nothing is more practical. A sound philosophy of society is the condition of all right conduct. The origin and value of philosophy, says a recent writer, is "in an attempt to give a reasonable account of our own personal attitude towards the more serious business of life. You philosophize when you reflect critically upon what you are actually doing in your world. What you are doing is, of course, in the first place living, and life involves passions, faiths, doubts, and courage. The critical inquiry into what all these things mean and imply is philosophy. We have our faith in life; we want reflectively to estimate this faith. . . . Whether we will it or no, we all of us do philosophize. . . . The moral order, the evils of life, the authority of conscience, the intentions of God, how often have I not heard them discussed, and with a wise and critical skepticism, too, by men who seldom looked into books!"[1] We all have our philosophical explanation of life; and it is of the utmost importance that it be a sound explanation, for all our conduct is shaped by it. Salvation can mean nothing more than help in realizing our own idea of life, unless it also involves help in understanding what life means. From what are we saved? From sin, is the orthodox answer. And what is sin? It is the transgression of the law, or want of conformity to the law. What law? The law of life. And the law of life is simply the expression of our relation to our environment, which is precisely what we have been talking about. We must have clear ideas about what that law requires of us before we can be saved from sin. The grace that bringeth salvation comes to help us to

[1] *The Spirit of Modern Philosophy*, by Josiah Royce, pp. 1, 2.

live according to the law of life. If any
man accepts the doctrine of individualism
or the doctrine of socialism as the correct
statement of the law of life, he will be praying for aid to conform his conduct to that
doctrine. If that doctrine is unsound his
conduct will be bad. There are millions of
people all over the world who are devoutly
praying for help in doing wrong. What
they need is not more religion, but a better
philosophy of life.

Every man has a philosophy of life. It
may be implicit rather than explicit; he
may not be able to formulate it; but there
are certain underlying principles which condition all his conduct, and it is of the last
importance that these principles be sound
and true.

Let me try to indicate with some particu-
larity just what the effect of a sound philosophy will be upon some phases of conduct.

1. In the experience of personal religion,
for example, how will the organic theory of
life be found to work?

The Christian man will not, under the influence of this theory, forget that he is a person; that his relations with the Father of spirits are primarily personal; that the responsibilities of life rest upon him, and cannot be evaded; that nobody can repent or believe for him; and that there is work in the kingdom of God which none but he can do. On the other hand, he will feel that in his deepest religious experiences he is not separated from his fellow-men, but identified with them. His chief happiness as a Christian will consist, not in inward raptures, but in the fellowship of the spirit. He will think very little about enjoying religion, and a great deal about the privilege and honor of service. His best evidence that he is a Christian disciple will not be in some ecstasy by which he is distinguished from his fellows, but in the knowledge that his deepest purpose is to seek first the kingdom of God.

Under the theory of individualism, which makes the supreme religious obligation the saving of one's own soul, great intensity of religious enthusiasm is often engendered, and the rapt saint finds high satisfaction in the indulgence of his emotions; but such experiences are no bar to an intolerant, exacting, overbearing temper; those who are most distinguished for their emotional exaltations are quite apt to be censorious and quarrelsome. This is precisely what we should expect; a theory of life which makes the individual the centre of the universe is not likely to bring peace and goodwill to his neighbors.

On the other hand, the socialistic theory so disparages the individual that the personal relations of men to God are wholly obscured, and the personal services of man to man are greatly undervalued.

2. This leads us to consider the effect upon our social conduct of the realization of the truth that we are members of one body. The man who really believes this will not, on the one hand, forget that the welfare of society depends on his individual action. He

will remember that the health and growth of the body depend upon the working in due measure of each several part. And yet he knows that it is only "in love" that the body is built up; that the coöperation of part with part, and the ministry of each to the good of all, is the very law of its being. If he were a socialist, he would expect to secure some new organization of society by which the good of all would be secured without effort or sacrifice on the part of any. If he were an individualist, he would say, in the words of one of them, that " every man and woman in society has one big duty: that is, to take care of his or her own self." But, being a Christian, he does not adopt the heresy of Cain, nor does he expect salvation by machinery. He knows that the welfare of the many is the fruit of the efforts and sacrifices of each one, and that the welfare of each one is found in the health and happiness of the many. He knows, in short, the truth of that saying which I have already quoted, that " the social organism can only exist as a structure of free individual wills, each entertaining the social purpose in an individual form." He must have his own power and use it, his own possessions and employ them, but all must be done for the welfare of the community with which his life is inseparably joined. He can never say, "This money is mine, and I shall do what I will with it;" that is not his conception of the function of money. Nor can he say, "This business is mine, and I shall manage it to suit myself;" business has quite another meaning to him. Money, as he has learned to think of it, is the chief instrument of beneficence; business is the great opportunity of social ministry. Office is not to him a chance for self-aggrandizement or plunder, but a call to consecrated service; learning is not a staff by which he climbs to heights where the multitude cannot follow, but a torch wherewith he lights the lowly paths of human kind; art is not a ministration to his selfhood, but a witness to the beauty which is the common

heritage of man. In short, he has learned
that the chief end of man is not the upbuild-
ing of one at the cost of the many, nor the
absorption of one in the life of the many,
but the perfection of one in the blessedness
of the many.

V.

THE SACRED AND THE SECULAR.

I know nothing which has exercised a more pernicious influence on religion than that unhappy divorce which has been effected between religious duty and the every-day duties of life. When a mother is faithfully tending her children, and making her hearthstone clean and her fire burn bright, that everything may smile a welcome to her weary husband when he returns from his work, it is never dreamt that she is religiously employed. When a man works hard during the day and returns to his family in the evening to make them all happy by his placid temper and quiet jokes and dandlings on the knee, the world does not think — perhaps he does not think him-self — that there is religion in anything so common as this. Religion is supposed to stand aloof from such familiar scenes. But to attend the church, to take the sacrament, to sing a psalm, to say a prayer, is religion. Now God help this poor sinful world if religion consists only in these things and not also in the other. — JOHN CUNNING-HAM, in *Scotch Sermons*, page 46.

We cannot expect the mass of men to take an interest in the technical parts of religion, in the details of the modes of worship, or the peculiar ways of expression, on which most controversies turn. These are the pro-fessional business of a class, — the ministers of public worship, the professed theologians. But every man, nay every human being, can learn to do his duty as in God's sight, and in the spirit of our Lord Jesus Christ; and the more each one is earnestly engaged in this effort, the more he will feel the need of the divine help, and the more he will lean with manly trust on the support of Christ and of the Holy Spirit. The contact of Christian faith with the secular life is good for both. The one is prevented from sinking into weak refinement, the other is raised from its grossness to become the temple of God. — W. H. FREMANTLE, *The Gospel of the Secular Life*, page 71.

THE SACRED AND THE SECULAR.

"I came not," said Jesus, "to judge the world, but to save the world." It may be well to pause in the middle of the last decade of the nineteenth century of the Christian era, and try to understand the meaning of these words of Jesus Christ,— "I came to save the world." It was a tremendous saying when it was first uttered by a Galilean peasant in the temple court at Jerusalem. How does it strike our minds to-day? Is its meaning any clearer now than it was then, or its promise any surer?

There are those who assume to be the special representatives of this Christ upon the earth, and who declare, if I rightly understand them, that the purpose of the Christ, as here announced, has not been fulfilled; that his lofty enterprise has met with ignominious failure ; that he has not saved the world, and gives no indication of being able to save it ; that, in spite of his church and his gospel and his spirit, the world is steadily growing worse ; that nothing is now left for Him but to reverse his original purpose and come and judge the world, and destroy what he is powerless, by moral and spiritual influences, to save. I will not discuss this theory ; I will only say that I do not find in history, nor in the philosophy of faith, nor in the words of Christ, anything to justify it. I still believe that when Christ said, " I came to save the world," He was no callow enthusiast, proposing to himself a scheme far too vast for his powers. I believe that He has not been disappointed ; that the joy that was set before Him was no illusion ; that He has shown himself mighty to save the world, and that the world through Him is being saved. And I own that the denial of this fact, or skepticism about it, seems to me the deadliest heresy now alive in the Christian church.

Others there are who interpret these words of Christ in a somewhat different sense. They do not dispute his power to save individuals out of the world, — many individuals ; perhaps they would admit that the day might come when all men would be converted. But this salvation of individuals, as they seem to conceive it, has no perceptible effect upon the physical world or the social world. Men are converted and brought into the church, which is the society of the regenerate, and from this time they cease to have any vital relations with the world. The world stands over against them in contrast, sometimes in antagonism ; the world is to be struggled against and overcome, but it is not to be saved. The whole framework of society — its industries, amusements, customs, governments, arts — is regarded as an alien and even a hostile kingdom. That Christ came to save this is an idea that a great many Christians have not entertained. Christ comes, as they suppose, to save men out of the world ; but

when these individuals are converted, their
trade, their politics, their institutions, their
fashions, their work, their play, still re-
main unsubdued by the influences of the
Spirit, — a realm of carnality and ungod-
liness.

It is rather difficult for any one who possesses a little imagination to conceive of
such a condition of things as this. The
fact being that all these social features are
the expression of the lives of individuals in
social relations, one finds it hard to understand how the people could all be saved
and the social order left untouched. It
seems a little like supposing that the warp
and the woof might both be changed from
hemp to silk and the web still be hempen,
or that the springs which feed the brook
might all be cleansed without purifying the
water of the brook. But the fact that a
conception is difficult is no stumbling-block
to some kinds of heroic faith. And it must
be admitted that this idea of a world left
substantially unaffected by the progress of

the church — a world out of which the
church is gathered, and with which it can
maintain no relations but those of hostility — is the notion which has dominated
the thought of the church through all the
generations.

Doubtless there are many passages of
Scripture which seem to support this theory. The free, popular, poetic use of language which we find in the Bible leaves
room for many misconceptions. I have no
time here to gather and analyze these passages. "The world," in some of them,
does signify the mass of unholy and anti-
Christian powers. The tenth definition of
"world" in the Century Dictionary is this:
"The part of mankind that is devoted to
the affairs of this life, or interested in secular affairs; those concerned especially for
the interests and pleasures of the present
state of existence; the unregenerate or un-
godly part of humanity." There are texts
of Scripture not a few, in which this definition would give the exact meaning. But

there are other texts in which this cannot be the meaning: "Ye are the light of the world." "The field is the world." "The gospel shall be preached in the whole world." "Go ye into all the world and preach the gospel to every creature." "God sent not his Son into the world to condemn the world, but that the world through Him might be saved." "God so loved the world that he gave his only begotten Son, that whosoever believeth in Him might not perish, but have everlasting life." "For the bread of God is that which cometh down from heaven and giveth life unto the world." In many such texts it is evident that the word is used to describe the human race, humanity, man and his environment; that it is not thought of as a hostile realm set over against the kingdom of heaven, but as the subject of Christ's redeeming and saving grace. And this is clearly the significance of the text before us. It is the world — the whole world, lying in wickedness now, but waiting with earnest expectation,

groaning and travailing together, for the
promised redemption ; it is the cosmos, riven
and shattered no doubt in many of its fair-
est tracts by chaotic forces, but still the
cosmos which sprang into being at first
from the mind and the heart of God — that
Christ came to save. And He has not failed
in doing what He came to do. He is saving
the world, the whole of it ; He is bringing
back lost Paradise ; his saving health is
known not only to individuals, but to nations, societies, institutions ; nay, it is even
true that his healing and transforming
power is felt in the physical world, and
that wherever He goes the wilderness and
the solitary place are glad for Him, and the
desert rejoices and blossoms as the rose.
When a man is saved from vice and ani-
malism, the signs of his regeneration are apt
to appear in the house which he inhabits ;
the new life will quickly make for itself a
new environment. It is quite as true of the
race as of an individual. The redemption
of man involves the redemption of the earth

whereon he dwells. Is not the physical world the subject of redemption? When we hear Paul explaining in the Epistle to the Colossians how the world came into existence, it seems not incredible that it should be redeemed. For he tells us that Christ, the image of the invisible God, is " the firstborn of all creation ; for in Him were all things created, in the heavens and upon the earth ; . . . all things have been created through Him and unto Him, and He is before all things, and in Him all things consist." The whole creation is fashioned in Christ ; his life permeates and animates it all ; it lives in Him. The immanence of God is a thought which has become familiar to devout thinkers, and it is a very fruitful conception. " Perhaps," says Canon Fremantle, " we may gain a more living conception of God by speaking of Him as the soul of the world, and comparing his action to that of the vital power of man upon his body ; or, in animated nature, to the action of the inner principle of life upon the parti-

cles of matter which make up the organism." This doctrine of God immanent in
nature needs to be supplemented, of course,
by the doctrine of God transcendent over
nature. But in this passage of Paul's we
have the explicit statement of the immanence of *the Christ* in creation: the Christ
idea, the Christ principle, — the substance
of that which Christ stands for and reveals
to us, — is part of the very framework of the
physical world, has been so from the dawn
of creation. This is the great thought
which Professor Drummond has so pow-
erfully presented to us in " The Ascent of
Man." With abundant learning, with marvelous eloquence, he shows us that when
man thought that

> " Nature, red in tooth and claw
> With raven, shrieked against his creed,"

he did not understand Nature; that love,
more than hate, is the song of her choiring
voices; that the struggle for life has for its
perpetual counterpart the struggle for the
life of others. Here is the Christ idea, the

Christ principle, imbedded in the very order of the physical world, precisely as Paul has told us. And if the creation has shared with man the losses and disorders which have resulted from his disobedience, it may also share with him in the redemptive and re-generative work which Christ has come to perform. It is not by its own will, for it has no will of its own, but by reason of its identification with man, that it has been subjected to vanity and misery; but Paul, with the insight of a spiritual imagination, beholds it waiting, with earnest expectation, for the day when it shall be manifest that men are the sons of God, because then the creation also shall be delivered from the bondage of corruption into the glorious liberty of the sons of God.

It is thus made evident that even the physical world is not a region foreign to the Prince of life; that the very love of which He was the incarnation is the element in which all things consist or hold together; and that the work of saving the world must include the renovation and the restoration of the natural as well as the spiritual order.

And if even the physical world is the subject of this redemptive work, much more must the framework of the social order be included in the redemptive process. The social framework, the customs, institutions, laws of society, are simply the organs by which the human race lives and has its being: the notion that men can be saved apart from these is something like the notion that a man who is sick can be made well while his heart and his brain and his lungs and his stomach and all the rest of his vital organs are fatally diseased.

The truth that Christ came to save the world must be accepted, then, in its largest sense. Any attempt to restrict his salvation to those interests which are expressed by the church as an ecclesiasticism is mischievous in the extreme. When you have fenced religion off into a separate realm, you have not only robbed society of the only power that can keep it from putrefaction, you have doomed religion itself to paralysis and death. The kingdom of heaven is the leaven which pervades the whole mass of society, and which is destined to bring, and which is bringing, the whole of life into harmony with the law of the spirit of life in Christ Jesus.

This brings us face to face with that separation of life into the sacred and the secular which lies at the basis of so much of our current thinking, but which is, in its common form, one of the most essentially irreligious ideas that the human mind can entertain. It goes back to the old Gnosticism, to the old Median and Persian Dualism; it has been working in the church from the earliest ages; it was the seed out of which monasticism sprung; it has seemed wellnigh impossible to rid the church of its baneful influence. This false distinction it was that underlay that papal hierarchy against which our fathers, in the early days of the Reformation, lifted up their protest. It was shutting religion into the church and out of the world that made the Reformation necessary. It was the sacerdotal ideas of that time against which William Tyndale, the translator of the Bible, was inveighing when he wrote : "For, since these false monsters crope up into our consciences, and robbed us of the knowledge of our Saviour Jesus Christ, making us believe in such pope-holy works, and to think that there was no other way into heaven, we have not wearied to build them abbeys, cloisters, colleges, chauntries, and cathedral churches with high steeples, striving and envying each other which should do most. And as for the deeds which pertain to our neighbors and to the commonwealth, we have not regarded at all, as things which seem no holy works, or such as God would not once look upon. And therefore we left them unseen to, until they were past remedy, or past our power to remedy them." [1] It was this church-cribbed, priest-centred religion against which the pulpit of Savonarola thundered, and the lecture-room of Colet rang,

[1] Deman's *Life of Tyndale*, p. 277.

and the pen of Erasmus flashed, in the open-
ing campaigns of that great controversy.
That Protestants should fall into this snare
is an instructive but not a very curious fact.
It is the law of the machine.   When Pro-
testantism succeeded in building up ecclesias-
ticisms of its own, it at once began to exalt
them above all the rest of life ; to separate
between them and all the rest of life ; to
regard them as holy and the rest of life as
profane.   That, to this day, is the prevailing idea.   It is not the universal idea, for
there are many in this generation to whom
the larger truth that Christ came to save
the world is becoming increasingly plain ;
but there still lingers, in the minds of the
majority of professing Christians, the notion
that religion is an interest wholly separate
from the rest of life ; that religion is sacred,
while business and politics and amusement
and education and art are essentially and
necessarily secular ; and that religion cannot
be brought into contact with these other interests without suffering some serious loss of

its own purity and dignity. The popular notions on this subject are not nearly so gross as once they were. We have got pretty well past that time which Dr. George Hodges describes in this stinging paragraph : —

" No man's sense of religion was affronted by the account given of the French cardinal, who was declared to be mean, cruel, avaricious, and dishonorable, but very religious. Benvenuto Cellini broke all the commandments, but attended the services of the church with regularity and devotion, and believed that his steps were guarded by the blessed angels. An honest, pure-hearted, God-fearing heretic, no matter how upright his life, would go to hell. But a loyal son of the true church, who recited the creed and knelt at the sacrament, might live most basely and yet have place hereafter with patriarchs and saints among the saved." [1] No such statement as that would hold good to-day in any branch of the church in this

[1] *The Heresy of Cain*, p. 11.

country. We are certainly making progress in our realization of the idea that personal religion cannot be separated from personal morality. But we still hold fast — many of us — to the notion that religion has a sphere to itself, and that the distinction between the church and the world must be maintained and emphasized; that a certain part of life is under religious motive, and that another and far larger part of life is under motives of another sort, and that the two realms cannot be brought together.

The truth is, that this distinction between the sacred and the secular is utterly misleading. What do we mean by the secular? If the essence of secularity is selfishness, greed, pride, cruelty, hardness of heart, there is plenty of all these in the church itself. Are not the competitive methods by which place and distinction in the house of God are sold for money essentially secular? Is not the pushing of the schemes of sectarian aggrandizement in our cities, in utter defiance of the comity of churches, a secular proceeding? Are not the politics of a good many of our ecclesiastical assemblies about as secular as any other kind of politics? When the mob spirit takes possession of a synod or a convention, and the rights of the minority are trampled under foot, and harsh judgments are rushed through, not by the force of reason but by the terrorism of the multitude, what name do we give to such an operation? It is not, surely, a sacred performance, even though it may take place in the very presence of the altar.

On the other hand, when an employer of men writes me, as one did a few weeks ago, "I have not reduced the wages of my men during the depression. There was a time when I was profiting largely by their work; now that it is otherwise I do not mean to forget what I owe them," — is that what you call a secular proceeding? And when a public-school teacher tells me of a boy in one of her classes whose habits and tendencies were thoroughly bad, but over whom she has succeeded in establishing an influence by kind treatment, by appeals to his manliness, until now he seems to be well started in the better way, shall I tell this young woman that work of this kind is merely secular? And when a prophet of God, in this dispensation, rises up and in the name of Jehovah smites the most gigantic aggregation of political injustice and corruption ever heaped together in one place upon this planet, and scatters it to the four winds of heaven, making a free space on which to build a government that shall be a shelter and not a terror to the people, — a shrine and not a slaughter-house, — shall we call him a secular preacher, and cry out that the function of the pulpit is not the preaching of politics, but the saving of souls?

In truth, there is no kind of work in which any man has a right to engage that is not in its deepest meaning sacred work. What is the farmer's work? He is developing the powers of the earth; he is causing it to bring forth and bud, that it may

give seed to the sower and bread to the
eater; he is working together with God.
What is the work of the miner? He is
bringing forth from the treasures of the
earth the stores of wealth that God has
been keeping there for his children; he is a
co-worker with God. What is the work of
the artisan or the manufacturer? He is
shaping the products of mine or field or for-
est for human uses; he is a co-worker with
God. What is the merchant's work? He
is bringing the goods that supply human
needs to the places where they are needed;
he is the helper of the farmer and the manufacturer; with them, he is a co-worker with
God. What is the work of the teacher?
In a more direct and conscious way he is
working with God; for, if he have any adequate idea of the meaning of his calling, he
knows that it is not merely or mainly for
bread-winning that he is training these
pupils, but that he is seeking to develop
their essential manhood and womanhood, —
to enable each one of them to become what

God meant him to be. What is the work of the physician? It is to make man, in the words of the Great Physician, "every whit whole." Is not he, too, working together with God? And what is the lawyer's function? Is it not, primarily, the right administration of the laws? And what are these laws of the state? Are they not in their final intention, in their deepest purpose, the effort to secure justice and righteousness among men? And is not this the purpose of the divine government? Must not the lawyer, therefore, feel that, when he gets into the heart of his calling, his work must be essentially religious, — that he must be a co-worker with God?

"Each of the various functions that we fill," says Canon Fremantle, "is a priesthood; the service which we render in them is a holy sacrifice; the materials which we employ are sacraments and signs of the spiritual act within. The student who devotes himself to the acquisition of truth, whose prayer is that his mind may be sustained

till he has acquired the knowledge which
it is his duty to seek, is ministering in a
sacred office, and his writings, up from the
simplest college essay or analysis to the
highest product of genius, the outward
working of his spirit within, are the emblems and signs of his ministry. The
trader who is determined to act honestly,
and who is conscious that his trade is a
means of benefit to others, and follows it
with that object, is a minister of God for
their good, and the commodities with which
he deals are the outward sign of his honesty
and his beneficence. The artist, whose object is beauty, is, by purifying and ennobling our sense of beauty, doing service to
God and man, and the works of his art are
the media by which his service is rendered.
. . . I need not point out that the same is
true in the family, where every father is a
priest by a kind of natural consecration;
nor in the state, where every ruler is a minister of God for our good. The great want
of our age is that we should look at all these

functions, not as profane and secular, according to the heathen and Jewish idea which Christ came to banish, but as those in which the service of Christ preëminently lies. There is the true sacrifice, there the living priesthood; there is the sacrament of our union, the real presence and the body of Christ our Lord." [1]

That all these common functions and callings are, when rightly understood and rightly performed, in the deepest sense sacred, is a fundamental truth of Christianity, yet it is a truth which has waited long for general recognition. Like the truth of the fatherhood of God and the truth of the brotherhood of man, it has been understood by a few in all the ages, and uncertainly and feebly held by the church at large, but its real meaning and significance have been practically hidden. Every one would say that the farmer ought to be a religious man; that is to say, he ought to keep the Sabbath, and go to church, and have family

[1] *The Gospel of the Secular Life*, pp. 190, 191.

prayers, and ask a blessing at the table, and
be a devout and prayerful person every day;
but that his work itself, — his plowing and
sowing and reaping is in itself coöperation
with God, and ought to be a conscious and
a joyful coöperation; that his work ought
to be full of the spirit of worship, — how
often has he heard any such truth as this?
So with all the other lawful callings which
men follow. The common conception is that
they furnish simply a means of livelihood;
they are just *secular*, that word tells it all;
in the words of the dictionary, they are " dissociated from, or have no concern with religious, spiritual, or sacred matters or uses."
That they can be thought of and used as
sacramental, — as the expression of love and
loyalty to God, — this, I say, is not a familiar conception. It ought to become familiar.
What an infinite pity it is that men cannot
gain some sense of the dignity and divine-
ness of common life! What a meaning is
imparted to existence when we are able to
see that in all the lowliest paths of human

service we are literally walking and working with God! Was not the poet's aim a noble one when he cried, —

> " By words
> Which speak of nothing more than what we are
> Would I arouse the sensual from their sleep
> Of death, and win the vacant and the vain
> To noble raptures "?

It is not needful to speak of more than what we are, — of more than what the humblest honest worker in the world is, and should know himself to be; that simple statement has enough inspiration in it to make the most prosaic life heroic and sublime.

And this, if I understand the matter, is what Christ meant when he said, "I came to save the world." He came to make all life divine. He came to bring us into such conscious nearness to God, into such living fellowship with Him, that we should be able to discern God's purpose in all our work, and to link our wills with his in a perpetual consecration, believing that whether we eat or drink, or whatever we do, we are doing all to his glory.

This new conception of Christianity is beginning to find expression in churches of a new type, with a greatly broadened ministry. There lies before me, as I write, the picture of a new and noble edifice recently erected in a Western city, and with it a full account of the kind of work which this church proposes to carry on, in the forty-two rooms that are covered by its roof. The contrast between the sacred and the secular finds no sanction here. For here, in addition to the ordinary provisions for public worship, are large facilities for interests that are usually regarded as secular. Here is a gymnasium, for physical culture and athletic training; here is the offer of a bicycle club, an athletic club, and a camera club, for outdoor pleasures; here are educational and industrial classes of various sorts: instruction in music, instrumental and vocal; in languages; in applied science, electricity, and microscopy; in commercial arithmetic and bookkeeping and penmanship; in mechanical and architectural drawing; in millinery; in white sewing; in dressmaking and in cooking; and a fine arts club, and a tourist club, and a reading-room, and recreation-rooms, with literary and debating societies; while lectures, concerts, and other entertainments complete for the present a programme which will undoubtedly be extended from year to year. For all these forms of work and enjoyment, this building, whose plan is before me, makes ample provision. There are rooms here, numerous, commodious, beautiful, in which this work may be carried forward. The church opens these hospitable doors, and expects and desires that the people of its neighborhood, rich and poor, will freely avail themselves not only of its privileges of worship, but of all these facilities of instruction and recreation. And it is a church that is doing all this, — a Christian church. And it is doing this because it is Christian, through and through; because it has entered into the

mind of Christ more intimately than most
churches do; because it understands what
He meant when He said, " I came to save
the world."

It may be surmised that these various ad-
ditions to the equipment of this church are
intended merely, or at any rate chiefly, as
attractions, — as baits; that their purpose is
to draw the people into the building, and
thus give the ministers and the evangelistic
workers a chance to convert them. It is to
be hoped, indeed, that a great many of those
who come will find something a little better
than they came for; some new view of the
meaning of life, which will lead them out
into a completer manhood and womanhood,
— into the liberty of the glory of the sons of
God. But after all, the idea that these features of the life of this church are simply
introduced as lures does not, I think, at all
represent the facts of the case.

The gymnasium has its place in this plan
because physical health and strength are
sacred possessions, gifts which God wishes

and works to bestow on all his children. It is because this church aims to be a co-worker with God that it furnishes the gymnasium. The recreation-rooms and the clubs for out-door sports are furnished for the same reason, because in God's plan rest must alternate with work, and recreation follow mental strain. This is not a secular provision; it is part of the divine order; and the church recognizes it and treats it as such. The classes for industrial education are offered because work before play is the divine ordinance; and the training which enables a man to work intelligently and skillfully is preparing him to fulfill the high calling of God. The laws of physics and mechanics, which underlie this industrial education, are only the ways in which God works; and the better a man understands God's ways and the more perfectly he conforms to them, the happier and the more successful he will be in every industrial calling. Of the sciences, which are to be taught in this place, exactly the same thing must be said, — the student

of every science is only thinking God's
thoughts after Him. Shall we call the study
of science a secular avocation? And the
music which is taught here, — are the voices
with which it speaks to the spirit secular
voices? Doubtless music, and all the arts,
may be perverted to a degree which shall require a much stronger word than secular to
describe their baseness; the best things can
be most desecrated; but rightly ministered,
music becomes the vehicle of the purest and
loftiest emotions, — the only language that
can express the aspiration of the soul that
thirsts for God, or the rapture of the bea-
tific vision.

And what shall we say of the large provision made for social intercourse, — for the
bringing of the people of the neighborhood
together in kindly and fraternal relations, —
that they may look each other in the face,
take each other by the hand, and manifest to
each other the goodwill which springs in the
hearts of all who have learned of Christ?
Is this a secular enterprise? Is the strength-

ening of the ties of friendship among neighbors a secular business? What will be the signs of the presence of the kingdom of heaven when it has fully come? Will they be anything other or better than peace on earth and goodwill among men? And is the work of the church in promoting on earth these heavenly relations anything less than sacred?

No; these instrumentalities, somewhat unusual in the equipment of a Christian church, are not furnished in any furtive fashion — as a kind of Christian cajolery to entrap and convert souls; they are provided for what they are worth in themselves; they are included as representing essential elements in the development and manifestation of the Christian life; they are offered because this church has gained a new conception of what Christ meant when he said, " I came to save the world." They are in this plan because this church has felt the meaning of such stirring words as these of Professor Drummond:

" The nearer one draws to reality, the

nearer one draws to the working sphere of religion. Wherever real life is, there Christ goes. And He goes there, not only because the great need lies there, but because there is found, so to speak, the raw material with which Christianity works, — the life of man. To do something with this, to infuse something into this, to save and inspire and sanctify this, the active working life of the world, is what He came for. Without human life to act upon, without the relations of men with one another, of master with servant, husband with wife, buyer with seller, creditor with debtor, there is no such thing as Christianity. With actual things, with humanity in its every-day dress, with the traffic of the streets, with gates and houses, with work and wages, with sin and poverty, with these *things*, and all the things and all the relations and all the people of the city, Christianity has to do, and has more to do than with anything else. To conceive of the Christian religion as itself a thing, — a something which can exist apart from life ; to think of it as something added on to being, something kept in a separate compartment called the soul, as an extra accomplishment like music, or a special talent like art, is totally to misapprehend its nature. It is that which fills all compartments. It is that which makes the whole life music and every separate action a work of art. Take away action, and it is not. Take away people, houses, streets, character, and it ceases to be. Without these there may be sentiment, or rapture, or adoration, or superstition; there may even be religion — but there can never be the religion of the Son of Man." [1]

And yet it must not be supposed that the other parts of this church are of no special value. I have dwelt upon its exceptional appointments, because I desired to enforce their significance and their sacredness; but the ordinary provision for worship, for the study of God's truth, for those acts and exercises which are the largest part of the life of all Christian churches, is not, in any

[1] *The City without a Church,* pp. 12, 14.

thought of mine, disparaged. The worship of such a church will be, indeed, less than nothing and vanity unless its life permeates and sanctifies all these common things ; but when its life does permeate and sanctify all these common things, then its sanctuary will be crowded and its prayer-rooms full to overflowing. When men begin to understand that they are walking and working with God six days in the week, when they comprehend that they have actual fellowship with the Father and with his son Jesus Christ in the humblest tasks to which they devote their powers, then they will find in the Sabbath worship a meaning which they have never known before. When the athlete, in the sanctified gymnasium, stands face to face with the fact that his body is the temple of the living God, he will feel it to be an unseemly thing if from that temple the incense of prayer never ascends to God. When the student, under the roof that shelters the altar, realizes that all his studies are but efforts to interpret the eternal Reason, his reverence must awaken a desire to know more fully the Being whose ways are thus in part revealed to him.

No, it cannot be that the realization of the sacredness of all life will rob our hearts of reverence or silence the voices of our praise. We must all come, led by a common impulse, to the altar of God, to God our exceeding joy, to pour out our hearts before Him, to confess our unworthiness of so great love, and to pray for the light and truth that shall lead us in his ways. When every calling is a priesthood, when every task is a prayer, the church bell will have a music in its peal that our ears have never heard. "Those," says Canon Fremantle, "who acknowledge that the sanction which makes their work a noble service is the belief in God, will want to hear more about God, and will return to theology and its teachings with a new zest." Thus there is reason to hope that the weekly assemblies of such a church will be thronged with earnest seekers after God, with men and women whose deepest wish is to know his will more perfectly, and to come into closer fellowship with Him.

Such a concrete example as this church furnishes — and there are not a few like it in the land — brings before us more clearly than much theorizing could do the nature of the changes which are taking place in the minds of men respecting the false distinction so long maintained between things sacred and things secular. I am persuaded that the new conception gives to religion a dignity and power which it has not known, and that it will greatly hasten the progress of the kingdom of God.

VI.

THE LAW OF PROPERTY.

Within the spheres of private industry and personal endeavor much service may be rendered in binding some men happily together : and in these relations there is no social obligation more constant or more imperative. Every manufacturer, every business man, has opportunity and divine calling within his own private business to serve the highest interests of society. The social obligations of men to men in their industries are not to be left out of the account, as though they belonged only to some conscienceless and loveless domain of economics, and not to the world of God's love. Whatever in the conduct of private business experience commends as profitable to prevent the proletarizing of a laboring class becomes an ethical responsibility and a Christian duty of the administrator and the capitalist. — NEWMAN SMYTH, *Christian Ethics*, page 463.

Now all her standards were spiritualized. She had come to know what happiness and affection are possible in three rooms, or two, on twenty-eight shillings a week ; and, on the other hand, her knowledge of Aldous — a man of stoical and simple habit, thrust, with a student's tastes, into the position of a great landowner — had shown her, in the case at least of one member of the rich class, how wealth may be a true moral burden and test, the source of half the difficulties and pains — of half the nobleness also — of a man's life. . . . She had ceased to think of whole classes of civilized society with abhorrence and contempt ; and there had dawned in her that temper which is in truth implied in all the more majestic conceptions of the state — the temper that regards the main institutions of every great civilization, whether it be property, or law, or religious custom, as necessarily, in some degree, divine and sacred. For man has not been their sole artificer ! Throughout there has been working within him "the spark that fires our clay." — MRS. HUMPHRY WARD, *Marcella*, ii. 487-489.

VI.

THE LAW OF PROPERTY.

THE moral education of the race has not been a gradual process, nor has it gone on by logical or ideal methods ; there has been a great want of symmetry and apparent coherency in the movement ; its course does not resemble the skillfully chosen line of the canal, but the devious channel of the river. If any social philosopher had planned the moral progress of humanity, it would have gone forward in a very different way. The anomalies and inconsistencies which appear at every stage of this progress would, of course, have been avoided. The logical absurdity of permitting this, while condemning that, would have been pointed out, and the race would have been taught that it was better to be symmetrically bad than unsymmetrically good.

There is reason, however, to doubt whether the pedagogy of the moral philosophers would have been more effective than that which has been conducted; perhaps the indirect and tentative methods of Providence are better calculated to reach sure results than the clever contrivances of men.

We are struck, in studying the moral education of the people who are, by common consent, the ethical leaders of the race, with the way in which moral conceptions were slowly naturalized among them. The great truth toward which they were to be led was the sacredness of all life; but the first step in that direction was the consecration of some small portion of life. To have told these people the whole truth would have been inexpedient; they could not receive it; a partial revelation was the only possible revelation. Some little part of life was separated from the rest and brought under the law of consecration. When they had learned something of the principle of consecration in this limited field, the time would come when it could be extended to wider realms.

The method, after all, commends itself to our judgment. When a small colony takes possession of a continent yet uncultivated, it is necessary that its first attempts to subdue the land be concentrated within narrow inclosures. The fact that the labor of the colonists is bestowed on a very few acres is no indication that their purposes may not include the land outside their fences. From these few acres as a base of operations they can extend their cultivation. The attempt to cover the whole continent the first year would not be practicable. And if the moral education of the Hebrew race began with the reclamation of some small tracts of conduct, the method was probably adapted to the intellectual condition of the people.

Thus, in the olden time, men were required to fast on certain days. Beyond a doubt, the ulterior purpose of this fasting was the control of the appetite, — the cultivation of temperance in the Scripture sense of the word. It would not have been possible to teach these people to rule their appetites every day, and at every meal; to make reason the arbiter of their dietary. But if occasional days were set apart, upon which, under severe penalties, they were forbidden to eat at all, they would learn, under this discipline, the lesson that the will could control the appetite, and this lesson could by and by be expanded into a broader principle.

In the old times certain localities were made sacred. The presence of God was to be looked for in those sacred places; it was only there that He could be approached. This localization of worship seems to us a crude method; but perhaps the mind could not have been concentrated upon the thought of God without the aid of these associations of locality. Do we not all feel the influence of such associations upon our own spirits in quieting and elevating our thoughts? It was only by that communion with God which was thus promoted that

men were enabled to entertain the larger
conception of his presence as filling all
space. The time at length arrived when
Jesus could say to the woman of Sychar:
" Believe me, the hour cometh when neither
in this mountain nor in Jerusalem shall
ye worship the Father. The hour cometh,
and now is, when the true worshipers shall
worship the Father in spirit and in truth,
for such doth the Father seek to be his worshipers."

A still more striking illustration of the
partialness of the rudiments of morality
among the Hebrews is the legislation intended to restrict the old custom of blood
vengeance. By that custom the accidental
as well as the intentional homicide was
doomed to death by the slain man's next
of kin. It was the religious duty of the
avenger of blood to take the life of one
who, by the merest accident, had slain his
kinsman. Now the Levitical law does not
forbid such vengeance, albeit it is nothing
less than murder. It merely regulates this

passion. It provides cities of refuge, to which the accidental slayer may flee. If the avenger of blood can overtake him before he reaches the city of refuge, he is authorized by the law to kill him. If the slayer comes forth from his asylum at any time before the death of the high priest who was in office when the accident took place, the avenger of blood may kill him. Not till this high priest dies is he free to go forth and be protected by the law from the avenger of blood. So feeble in those old times was the sense of the sacredness of human life, so strong was the impulse of an irrational vengeance. To our moral sense the wrath of the avenger of blood seems only the impulse of a brute. Yet it is not prohibited; it is only moderated. Certain conditional safeguards are provided for the accidental slayer. These are designed to suggest to the seeker of vengeance that his passion needs restraint. The idea is insinuated into his mind that human life is too sacred to be the prey of mere insensate fury.

To the wild beast in him the law sets metes
and bounds, saying, Thus far, and no far-
ther. And doubtless this very legislation
did tend to check blood vengeance, and to
cultivate in the Hebrew mind the true ethical idea respecting human life.

It was precisely in this way that the doctrine of property was taught in those early
times. The consecration of their possessions to God was, as the Hebrews understood it, a very partial consecration. One
tenth of what they had rightfully belonged
to God, the other nine tenths belonged to
themselves. That was the provision of
their law. Doubtless it was a wise provision. The thin end of the wedge must be
used in riving the covetousness of the human heart. If men could be trained to
regard one tenth of their gains as belonging
to their Maker and set apart for holy uses,
that was as much, probably, as they would
willingly yield. The principle was established that their property was not all their
own; that other motives than those of self-

interest must control the disposition of a portion of it. As they learned the doctrine of the divine omnipresence by the consecration of sacred places ; as their first lessons in keeping fast days led them on toward the virtue of self-control ; as the restrictive regulations about homicide taught them the sacredness of human life ; so these very rudimentary lessons in the consecration of property prepared the way for that larger conception which Christianity was to introduce, under which the man who gives himself to God no longer considers that any portion of his estate, be it nine tenths or one tenth, is left out of the transaction.

I am not denying that there may be many persons in these days to whom the Jewish rule would be a helpful rule. So little conception have they of the real relation between themselves and the Father of their spirits, so utterly far away and foreign does He seem to the affairs of their every-day lives, that they cannot bring themselves to recognize any real partnership with Him in

things which they designate as secular.
Religion, as they understand it, is in interest wholly separate from business. The
motives which hold sway in the one realm
are spiritual motives, and those which hold
sway in the other realm are secular motives.
Their relations with God are wholly on the
religious side of their lives; the world is
a region with which He has nothing to do.
When they desire to commune with God,
they leave the world behind them; "what
part has He," they ask, "in those purely
secular affairs? We shall offend Him if
we bring any thought of them into the sanctuary." Much less is there any place for
Him and the high and holy affections which
He inspires in that workday world, with
whose business for six sevenths of our time
we must be engrossed.

To one who habitually regards all the
great and absorbing interests of life, and
especially those interests which have to do
with property, as secular and not sacred, the
proposition to take one tenth part of these

interests over into the other realm and con-
secrate them to God, is in the line of
progress. The man who acknowledges the
divine control of one tenth of his property
is nearer right than the man who thinks
that his property is all exclusively his own,
and that the divine purpose has nothing
to do with the disposition of it. The idea
of stewardship has found a lodgment in his
mind. The leaven is there; perhaps it will
gradually affect the whole lump.

· The Jewish rule of consecration may
therefore be a very good practical rule for
many persons in these days who profess and
call themselves Christians, just as there may
be many who would be profited by abstain-
ing from food periodically, as a reminder to
their unruly appetites that reason ought to
control them. But the rudimentary Jewish
rule ought not to be considered as the sufficient rule of Christians in this day of grace.
For even as the law of fasting was the first
step in the path to a control of all the bodily
appetites, and as the recognition of sacred

places led to the knowledge of the truth that
the whole earth is the temple of the living
God, and as the checking of the avenger's
fury at the gates of the city of refuge opened
to him the truth that the life of man is precious in the sight of God, so this institution
of the tithe was the initial stage in that discipline by which men were to be taught
that all their property is rightly held only
as a trust from the Infinite Goodness.

A clear-minded and conscientious man,
who had been reading a certain book, said
to me not long ago, " That chapter on property I cannot understand. The definition
by Dr. Brownson, of which a good deal is
made, conveys no idea to my mind. ' Property is communion with God through the
material world.' I do not know what that
means." I had no time to finish the conversation, but the remark has often recurred to
me. There must be something inadequate
about the phrase, or else my friend would
have got some meaning out of it. Perhaps the word " communion," with its litur-

gical association, was the stumbling-block. But the very first definition of communion, in the latest dictionary, is " participation in something held in common ; fellowship." Partnership would come nearer to conveying the legal meaning ; but I dare say that the theologian who framed the definition wished to keep as far away as possible from conceptions purely legal, and to emphasize the spiritual facts in the case, and therefore wrote " communion " rather than " partnership." But it seems to me that there ought to be no difficulty in entertaining the idea that we do, in very deed, through all our use of material things, enter into fellowship with God.   To one who believes that God is immanent in nature ; that all the natural forces are only modes of his activity ; that all living things live and move and have their being in Him, the idea cannot be very remote that we never touch the material world without coming into vital relations with Him.   Whatever we may have honestly accumulated, be the same little or much, we have gained by coöperating with Him. If our wealth has been won by developing the natural resources of the earth, we have been using his power every day. If it is the fruit of honest trade, our success has depended wholly on the observance and use of those social laws which He has impressed upon the human race. He has made men for society; He has made them to be members one of another and to help one another; and honest trade is nothing but a mutual exchange of services, by which the welfare of all is increased. The social laws which underlie all exchanges are the expression of the divine purpose concerning man; and he who makes good use of them, if he understands what he is about, knows that he is in fellowship with God.

Not otherwise is it with any productive or useful occupation. I do not say with every occupation, for there is much that men call work which is not worthy to bear that sacred name. A man may be, many a man is, in his daily employment fighting against God. He who seeks to aggrandize himself by perverting the powers of nature, by turning her wholesome fruits to poisons, by contriving ministries to depraved appetites, by pandering to destructive vices, by employing the forces of the earth to promote the degradation of men, is, in his habitual activity, in deadly enmity against God. The gains which he thus accumulates are not in any true sense property. The laws may recognize his title to them, for laws are not always able to express the essential righteousness; they are only approximations to the standard which, in our hearts, we accept. We are compelled to administer our jurisprudence in a manner which corresponds but roughly to the ideal of justice. But the possessions which a man has won by such practices as I have described are much more properly regarded as spoils or booty. They are the fruit of an insidious and destructive warfare against humanity.

Equally hostile to all divine fellowship is the work which sets at nought the truth of human brotherhood, and uses men as count-

ers in the game of life, or as tools in the
building of fortune. There are many to
whom the problem of life is the exploitation
of their neighbors. There are many to
whom business and politics are simply a
struggle for mastery, with woe to the van-
quished. The brother man by their side is a
stepping-stone for the ambitious to mount
by; if they would rather not prostrate him
in the process, it is mainly because while he
is erect they can mount higher by standing
on his shoulders. But the warfare of interest is relentless; the contestant counts all
whom he employs or with whom he deals
as lawful prey : his problem is to get from
his fellow-men as much as he can, and to
give them as little as he can; what becomes
of them is a question that he does not permit himself to consider. Do not understand
that I am ascribing purposes like these to
all the men in the active contests of life;
that would be a gross slander. I am not
willing to admit that the majority of the
men with whom we come in contact are of

this character: my impression is that the humane and the honorable and the fair are in the ascendant, both in numbers and in power. But it would be idle to try to conceal from ourselves the terrible truth that there are thousands among us who are ready to enrich or aggrandize themselves by poisoning the very sources of the national life. For the love of money, how many there are who will offer bribes, and thus help to break down the honor and integrity of voters and officials; and how many, on the other side, who will accept bribes, and use places of public trust for their own emolument. What fearful inroads are thus made upon the national virtue by unscrupulous wealth and wolfish ambition.

And there are many others, who push their industrial and commercial combinations in a manner so selfish, so oppressive, so tyrannical, that their whole work tends to destroy the sympathy and goodwill which makes society possible. So reckless are they of the rights of competitors and employees, so bent on crushing rivalry and elevating themselves upon the ruins of other fortunes, that their whole path through life is strewn with blasted hopes and marked by desolated homes ; and the only flowers that bloom by the wayside over which they have passed are the nettles and the brambles of resentment and ill-will. Dire and deadly is the work of these destroyers. The social conditions which they engender must be such as will tend to the disintegration of the social tissue and to the downfall of the social order.

It is hardly necessary to say that those whose work, however useful it might be in itself, is prosecuted in this spirit, are not working with God ; that they are simply laboring to pull down and destroy the work of God upon the earth. For even as there is no more real fellowship with God than that which the man rightfully enjoys who is doing good work with a good will, so there is no kind of opposition to God which is more positive or malignant than that of the

man who is using natural forces or social
opportunities in such a way as to degrade
his fellow-men, or to weaken the bond of
confidence and mutual regard by which they
are held together in society. The man who
blasphemes and denies God is not so dangerous a foe as the man who, it may be with
pious words upon his lips, is building up his
fortunes by methods which naturally involve
the hardening of his neighbors' hearts, the
ruin of their souls, and the increase of ill-
will among men. To speak of property
thus gained as in any sense sacramental —
as the medium through which the man holds
communion with God — would be little better than blasphemy.

But the great majority of our neighbors,
as I have said, are animated by no such
unsocial purposes. They are often more
thoughtless than they ought to be of the
welfare of those with whom they deal, but
their honest intention is on the whole benevolent ; they desire to live and let live ;
they would cry out with the poet : —

" Rich through my brethren's poverty ?
　　Such wealth were hideous : I am blest
　Only in what they share with me,
　　In what I share with all the rest."

And those who are carrying on an honest work in a spirit truly social are surely, in a most real sense, working together with God. Their gains have been made by entering into his designs, by thinking his thoughts after Him, by using the instruments and powers which He has furnished to their hands. The "Silent Partner" in all their labor has been the great Creator. Every day of their lives his presence has been with them, and his omnipotence has been the fund of power on which they have steadily drawn. The genial warmth of the sunbeams, the nourishing moisture of the earth, the unfailing pull of gravitation that moves the river currents downward, the rush of the compelling vapor, the heat of the coal, the energy of the electric spark, are all parts of his ways, witnesses to the ever present might of Him without whom we can do nothing. And when one has, in some good measure, accepted His wisdom as the guide of his endeavors, and has said, in humble recognition of His right to rule our lives, —

"Our wills are ours, we know not how,
 Our wills are ours to make them thine,"

must not the truth that property is communion with God through the material world become a very real thought to him? Will he have any difficulty in understanding that the gains which he has made, be they more or less, have been made in a life-long partnership with the Author of his being? To dispute it would be like the June garden proclaiming that with all its wealth of color the light had had nothing to do, or like the rainbow denying that the sun and the shower had any part in building its glowing arch.

So deeply seated in the very foundations of our ethical and spiritual being are the rights of property. Of all these profound conceptions jurisprudence can take no notice; that part of our being by which we are allied to God is beyond the reach of jurisprudence. Yet it is in these deep conceptions that we must always find the guiding lights of conduct. It is only when we realize our relations to the Power which is behind all phenomena that we know what duty means, and what are the true definitions of our rights.

If, then, I have anything that is rightfully mine, it is because He who gave me personality has been aiding me to realize my personality in the possession and use of material things. Nothing is mine apart from Him; everything that I rightly call my own I am holding and using with a reverent regard for his holy will.

When this conception gets naturalized in one's mind, and his habitual thinking adjusts itself to it, the old discussions about tithes will have been left very far behind. There is no need of taking a fraction, greater or less, and consecrating it to the service of the kingdom; the fundamental assumption is that it all is consecrated.

When the man reflects on how he came by it, he cannot set up any exclusive claim to it. The rights of the Silent Partner can never be ignored. And the question how this property can be dispensed is a question which can never be discussed without constant reference to the heavenly Father's will.

It may be supposed that such a conception would call for the bestowment of all we have in almsgiving and charitable work. But this by no means follows. I can conceive that a man might not give one dollar in what is known as charity, and yet might use his whole wealth in consecrated ministries. If a man employs his capital in business, and makes the law of that business the law of service, — seeking to make it useful in every way to those whom he supplies and to those whom he employs, seeking to fill all his relations to his associates and his neighbors with the spirit of Christ, — that dispensation of his property may be the most perfect form of communion with God which he could possibly devise. I do not believe that any more charitable, any more divine use of money can be thought of than that which is involved in the furnishing of honest and healthful work, and in the manifestation, through the friendships which association in work makes possible, of the true spirit of brotherly love. The man who can gather men about him in some productive industry, and can thus enable them by their own labor to earn a decent livelihood, and can fill all his relations with them with the spirit of Christ, making it plain to them that he is studying to befriend and help them in every possible way, is doing quite as much, I think, to realize God's purpose with respect to property, and to bring heaven to earth, as if he were founding an asylum or endowing a tract society.

There are those who conceive that any man of wealth whose will is in harmony with God's will must needs give a great deal right and left to all who ask for it. But this is not clear. It should be remembered that He to whom the wealth of the world belongs does not dispense it in this way. It must be that He has the power to take the wealth of the rich from them and distribute it among the poor. Yet this is not done. There must be some good reason why it is not done. I think that any man who tries to give away much money, and who watches its effect upon the recipients, will find out the reason. It is the hardest thing in the world to do good with money. The lavish, unconsidered bestowal of it upon all who seem to be in need is a very injurious business. The harm that is done by such a dispensation far outweighs the good. And the man whose property brings him into communion with God, and who seeks to conform all his expenditure to the will of God, will often be constrained to check his lavish impulses, and to give only so much as shall serve to stimulate the manhood and arouse the self-respect of the recipient.

It may be said that the conception of

this discourse, that property is only rightly held and used when man's partnership with God is acknowledged, is too high and fine for ordinary human beings; and that some less radical maxim would be more influential. I do not think so. It seems to me that we cannot afford to place before our minds any rule except the perfect rule. When we are legislating for states, we must consult expediency; when we are settling the principles of our own conduct, we must confront the ideal. And I do not believe that this principle is too bright and good for human nature's daily food. Indeed, there are signs on every hand that many men, who make but little parade of religion, are waking up to a solemn sense of their responsibility for the use of their property and their social opportunities. The idea that God is in his world, that he is really here with us, every day, that we live and move and have our being in Him, that He is not, so to speak, a merely Sunday God or a God of the sanctuary and the altar and the closet, but an every-day Friend, Companion, Counselor, Partner, Helper, one with whom our relations are more constant and more intimate than they can be with any other being, — this idea is beginning to get hold of the minds of men; and when they are once possessed by it, this will be a very beautiful world: its meanings will wonderfully expand; its horizons will widen; and the azure overhead will bend down to us like a benediction.

VII.

RELIGION AND POLITICS.

.

The elements which are manifest in the government of the nation, in its moral being, can have only a divine ground. The power which is in the people forming the nation is over the people; and while the individual acts in the government of the nation, it is over the individual and he is subject to it; and this is a power which is and can be in the nation only as it is a moral person and is derivative from God. This alone in government is the condition also of the reconciliation of law and freedom. The character of the authority of the nation also indicates its origin. It has authority, and is invested with power in the maintenance of a moral order on the earth. But the right thus to maintain authority over men belongs in itself to no man and no collection of men, and is existent in the nation only as it has a divine genesis. . . . The ruler who recognizes and follows only the popular voice and the popular opinion becomes himself a slave. And he only is truly a ruler and truly free who recognizes in the sovereignty of the nation this divine source of its unity and power, and whose action in it is therefore in immediate responsibility to God. — ELISHA MULFORD, *The Nation*, chapter iv.

Government, like man himself, participates of the divine being, and, derived from God through the people, it at the same time participates of human reason and will, thus reconciling authority with freedom, stability with progress. — ORESTES A. BROWNSON, *The American Republic*, page 126.

VII.

RELIGION AND POLITICS.

WHEN the line of division is run through life between things sacred and things secular, politics is always found on the secular side. In the common conception, that realm of human conduct is essentially and hopelessly profane. It may be admitted that there are good men in politics, but it is almost an axiom that politics themselves are irretrievably bad. I think that the average citizen feels that public life is in its very nature unholy; that any one who permits himself to be entangled with the affairs of state is by that contact almost sure to be defiled. If men do keep themselves pure in that service, it is by heroic resistance against evil tendencies, which are not only inseparable from it, but which are elements of the work itself. Of course it is not any

deep or serious thinking that comes to such
conclusions, but the popular estimate is
something like this. And it is certain that
the conception of the service of the state as
in any respect sacred is utterly foreign to
the mind of the average American citizen.
That seems, now that I have written it
down, a hard saying, but I cannot modify it.
Politics is, in the common conception, as
near to being completely "dissociated from
religious, spiritual, or sacred matters or
uses" as anything not criminal in this wide
world could be.

I wish to show that this common conception is totally and even horribly erroneous.
I would like to make it appear that there
is no particular in which the common conception of life or duty is in more urgent
need of modification than in this. If there
is any function fulfilled by man which is
essentially sacred, it is citizenship in a
republic; it is that which is involved in
the services of the state.

When we look in the Gospels for light

upon this question, we seem to find very little. The references of our Lord to political
affairs are few; chief among them is his
saying, " Render therefore to Cæsar the
things that are Cæsar's, but to God the
things that are God's." The fact that these
references are so few is often cited as a reason why ministers of our day should let political subjects alone. But the condition of
the people among whom Jesus was living
differed radically from those of our own
country. The Jews, in the time of Christ,
were a subject people; they were not, in any
important sense, a self-governing people.
They had no share in the administration of
their own national affairs. They had really
but two political duties, — to submit to the
Roman government and to pay their taxes.
It is said, in the narrative to which allusion
has been made, that two parties, the Pharisees and the Herodians, were trying to en-
tangle Jesus by their questions; but these,
so far as the government was concerned,
were simply cliques or coteries; they were

not political parties, that divided the power between them; neither of them had any hope of getting possession of the government except by revolution. All that was left to a Jew in the time of Christ was to endure the Roman rule, and to pay the tax-gatherer. These duties Jesus enjoined.

There had been a time when the Jewish nation was independent; when it was responsible for its own government; and then the air was always ringing with the political preaching of the prophets.

" The Jewish church," says Dr. Hodges, " was the Jewish nation. The prophets were patriot orators, who preached politics with vehemence, and entered might and main into public life. It is impossible to think of Isaiah as a quiet parish priest, living at the centre of a narrow circle, letting the great world outside go uninterrupted on its own mistaken way. In New York, in Boston, Isaiah would have been the heart and soul of a great, outspoken, radical, independent, righteous newspaper. Amos and Hosea would have put themselves in peril of the police by inflammatory speeches on the street corners and in the parks. All these men were interested in public questions profoundly and supremely. The saints of that time were the national heroes. They were the men who had done heroic service for the country. . . . These were the sacred names upon their church calendar. The leaders of the synagogue had been the guides of the national councils; and their sons, who sat upon the front seats in their fathers' places, were eager to emulate their patriotism and their valor. There was no difference between a parliament and a prayer-meeting. Any political question was also a religious question; into which excellent condition, though in a more Christian spirit, may we come ourselves." [1]

It was after this manner that religion and politics were blended in Israel, when the nation had a life of its own, and the prophets were the leaders of the people. Doubtless

[1] *The Heresy of Cain*, pp. 171, 172.

it would have been so now, if there had been
any laws to make or any offices to fill, or
any political duties to perform. Jesus did
not preach politics to the Jews of his day
for a very obvious reason. He would not,
I dare say, have preached against slander to
a congregation of mutes, nor against dancing
to a congregation of cripples. If the Jews
had had the government of their country in
their own hands, is it probable that He would
have had nothing to say about the way they
administered it? Read his arraignment of
the Scribes and Pharisees, and judge.

"Render to Cæsar the things that are
Cæsar's." Pay your taxes and obey the laws.
This was all they could do, and this He bade
them do. The government was far from
perfect; it was in many ways unjust and
oppressive : but a bad government is better
than anarchy ; in a rough way it preserves
order and prevents crime. Even Cæsar —
even the unspeakable Tiberius then upon
the throne — stood for something sacred
and venerable, and respect and obedience

must be paid to him as the representative of rightful power in the world. " Render therefore to Cæsar the things that are Cæsar's."

There is a sense in which this admonition of our Master may apply to Americans. In a certain way we, the people of this country, are persons under authority. The laws of the land are, in their totality, expressions of the national spirit ; and they are entitled to be regarded by all citizens with veneration. The laws are supreme. To them we yield submission and loyal obedience. The officers of the law, the magistrates, the judges, the governors, the persons who are called to represent and administer the law, stand, while they are in office, in a position of dignity and responsibility ; and so long as they are not evidently attempting to annul or defeat the law, so long as they are really identified with it, and are seeking to maintain it, we owe them respect and coöperation. There is, then, an important sense in which this command of Christ's, which enjoins submission and respect to lawful authority, is applicable to American citizens. The fact is not to be lost sight of that the citizens of a republic occupy a double position, — that they are subjects as well as sovereigns. A self-governing people is governed. It must know how to obey as well as how to command. The subordination must be as spontaneous as the franchise is free.

But there are many occasions in a republic when the maxim of Christ now before us does not express the deepest fact in the life of the American citizen. " Render to Cæsar the things that are Cæsar's " is a commandment which considers us as subjects of government; it bids us render to all their dues, — " tribute to whom tribute is due, custom to whom custom, fear to whom fear, honor to whom honor." But on election day, and on every occasion when the citizen contemplates the duties and responsibilities which culminate on election day, the citizen is not merely a subject, he is a sovereign.

" The proudest now is but my peer,
 The highest not more high ;
To-day, of all the weary year,
 A king of men am I.

"To-day alike are great and small,
 The nameless and the known ;
My palace is the people's hall,
 The ballot box my throne."

This is no sentimental exaggeration ; it is the statement of an exact, scientific, legal fact. The sovereignty resides in the body of the citizens, and nowhere else : they are the sovereign people. It is not my duty to Cæsar that I am thinking about on election day, — or any day in the year when I consider the nomination of candidates or the election of officers ; for 1 stand in Cæsar's place ; I sit on Cæsar's throne ; it is Cæsar's duty that rests upon my conscience ; and I am taking part in that august transaction on which the prophet was looking when he wrote : " Behold, a king shall reign in righteousness and princes shall rule in judgment."

Not our duty to Cæsar, but the duty of

Cæsar himself, the duty of ruling the land righteously, — this is the obligation that rests on every voter in a republican government. "The powers that be, are ordained of God." And who in a republic are "the powers that be"? Not, clearly, the officials; they are simply the employees, the servants of the sovereign. Their power is delegated. They receive it at the hands of the voters. The voters are the sovereigns. It is with them that the final responsibility rests. It is they who are ordained of God to establish justice, to defend liberty, to promote the common welfare. There is no power but of God; and those with whom the sovereignty rests in any nation, those who are actually clothed with it, must know that they are ordained of God to rule in his stead, to know his will, and to do it here upon the earth. Citizenship in a republic can mean nothing less than this. Not more surely was David, in the olden time, chosen and anointed by Jehovah to rule Israel than every American voter, in these days, is chosen and anointed by the Lord of Hosts to rule this land.

There are people in this country who count it a religious thing to refrain from taking any part in the government of the country. They say that the Christian has no right to meddle with politics; that Christ's kingdom has nothing to do with the kingdoms of this world. This is nothing but flat rebellion against the express command of God, who bids every ruler to rule with diligence.

Surely there must be government upon the earth. There are theoretical anarchists, but their numbers are few, and their theories are provisional merely; they hope that the world may be governed in such a way that by and by it shall not need to be governed at all. But meanwhile it must be governed. And for this government somebody must be responsible. In an absolute monarchy only one man is supposed to be responsible; if he accepts the responsibility, and his subjects assent, well and good; it rests with him, and he becomes the representative of God in the world, ordained and commissioned for the establishment of justice, the preservation of liberty, the promotion of welfare among his people. But in a republic the case is different. Here is no hereditary ruler ; here are no permanent office-bearers. Yet in this government the responsibility must rest somewhere. On whom does it rest ? Not surely upon the persons who are temporarily holding office. Their tenure of power is too limited and too slight to be charged with such a wide-reaching and permanent obligation. Obviously, it must rest upon the whole body of voting citizens. To them all the power is committed. They are the sole depositaries of the sovereignty. They are responsible, jointly and severally, for good government. If God has ordained any " powers that be " in this land, the voters must be these " powers." The ultimate and responsible sovereignty can be located nowhere else but in them. It is not a matter of

choice with them whether they will exercise
it or not; they are born into it; it belongs
to them, and they cannot divest themselves
of it. It is not a matter of choice with me
whether I will be the brother of my brother
or the son of my father. Those relations
were settled for me. It is not a matter of
choice whether a man who is born in this
free country will share the responsibility
for the government of this country. When
the time of his majority comes, that burden
rests upon him. If Paul's doctrine about
rulers is true, it is God who has laid it upon
him. For him to say that he will not accept it is simply rebellion against God.

To every citizen, then, these political duties are imperative and sacred. Up to the
high places of the kings, up to the level of
the thrones, these solemn obligations sum-
mon us all. In the choice of magistrates,
in the selection of representatives, we must
hear the voice of the King of kings, bidding
us arise and gird ourselves with power for
the great act of sovereignty. Such anoint-

ing as is implied in the investiture of citizenship should make every man sober, thoughtful, and humble. How can any man stand in the presence of a responsibility so great without deep searchings of heart!

> " Look from the sky,
> Like God's great eye,
> Thou solemn moon, with searching beam,
> Till in the sight
> Of thy pure light
> Our mean self-seekings meaner seem.

> " Shame from our hearts
> Unworthy arts,
> The fraud designed, the purpose dark;
> And smite away
> The hands we lay
> Profanely on the sacred ark."

We have a service, in some of our churches, preparatory to the sacrament of the Lord's Supper, and we are wont to spend some hours of reflection and prayer in making ourselves ready worthily to enter into that solemn service. It will be regarded by many as an extravagant saying, but I am speaking out of my deepest conviction, when I say that there is quite as much need of a deep and genuine religious preparation for the discharge of all the more important duties of citizenship. No man has any right to go to the political convention or to the polls; no man has any right to take in his hand the ballot, on which he will record his judgment respecting the government of the city or the state or the nation, until he has purged his heart of every particle of self-seeking, of every vestige of partisanship; until he is sure that he has put away from him all small piques and passions and all suggestions of personal interest in making his decision; until he knows that his supreme wish is to promote the glory of God, by promoting the highest good of the whole people. "Search me, O God, and know my heart: try me, and know my thoughts: and see if there be any wicked way in me, and lead me in the way of the eternal righteousness." If there is any time in his life when a good man needs to offer this prayer, it is when he confronts the high responsibilities of citizenship.

It is true, then, that Jesus had very little to say about politics, for the simple reason that the people to whom He was always speaking had nothing to do with politics. But suppose that He had been standing every day in the presence of Cæsar himself; suppose that his daily walk had led Him over to the Palatine Hill in the Eternal City, when the brutal Tiberius was dwelling in the splendid palace of Augustus; and that this proud emperor, fountain of political authority, sovereign over the greater part of the then known world, had been confronted from time to time by Him who claimed to be the Messiah of God: — can it be imagined that Jesus would have had nothing to say to this powerful monarch concerning his duty as a ruler? Can it be believed that the cruelty and extortion of the Roman rule would have gone unrebuked, that its corruption would have received no censure, that its prostitution of liberty and justice for gain would have called forth no protest? Would not this despot have been bidden with the voice before which Pilate quailed and trembled, to do justly, and to love mercy, and to walk humbly before God? What else would the Lord himself have said than that which the prophets, speaking in his name, had many a time spoken to kings and princes? Might we not have heard Him quoting, as so often He quoted, from Isaiah the prophet: "How is the faithful city become an harlot! she that was full of judgment! righteousness lodged in her, but now murderers. Thy silver is become dross, thy wine mixed with water. Thy princes are rebellious, and companions of thieves; every one loveth gifts and followeth after rewards: they judge not the fatherless, neither doth the cause of the widow come unto them. O my people, they which lead thee cause thee to err, and destroy the way of thy path."

With some such words of reproof and admonition we may be sure that He to whom all the prophets bore witness would have preached righteousness to the rulers, if rulers then had been in the audiences to which He preached. And if He were speaking, in these days, to the audiences in our churches, which are so largely made up of rulers, I cannot have any doubt as to what would be the tenor of his message. That He would preach politics, in the narrow acceptation of that term; that He would advocate the platform of any political party, or signify his preference among candidates, who represent nothing but party cries and catch-words, — no one for a moment supposes. But that He would impress upon all those listening to Him the sacredness and solemnity of the responsibilities resting upon them to rule righteously and in the fear of God; to put far away from them all thoughts of personal gains; to seek, in the supreme exercise of the sovereignty intrusted to them, the kingdom of God and his righteousness, is not, I think, an open question. And no man who speaks in his name has any right to suppress the message. The pulpit is not the place for partisan politics. But the pulpit is the place for enforcing upon the consciences of citizens the solemnity and the sacredness of the obligations which rest upon them, and their duty to discharge these obligations, as the Prayer Book says of another great engagement, — "reverently, discreetly, advisedly, soberly, and in the fear of God."

No one who has any adequate sense of existing political conditions will be inclined, I think, to censure the intensity of the plea here made for a view of political life and action which lifts it completely above the clamor and strife of the partisan assemblies into the screner air of the mountain-tops, where men stand face to face with God. For I am as sure as I can be of anything, that there is no salvation for this land of ours from the rising flood of factional strife and corporate greed, which threatens to engulf

our liberties, save in the heightened sense
of the sacredness of the vocation with which
every citizen is called. Many expedients
for improving political morality are pro-
posed, some of which are undoubtedly wise:
Australian ballots, corrupt practices acts,
proportional representation, the referendum,
civil service reform, — all of them worthy
of thought, but, after all, the fundamental
need is a deeper conviction, in the heart of
the citizen, of the truth that citizenship de-
mands a consecrated spirit, a heroic self-
denial, which shall make all the interests of
business and all the motives of self-aggrandizement subordinate to the welfare of the
nation.

It seems, indeed, almost quixotic to speak
or think of cleansing the filthy pool of
party politics: of infusing into the reservoir
of low aims and selfish schemes and mean
motives the clarifying power of a holy purpose. And, indeed, there are hours when it
appears that the whole temper of the time is
sordid and superficial and profane.

" Our slender life runs rippling by, and glides
 Into the silent hollow of the past;
  What is there that abides
 To make the next age better for the last?
  Is earth too poor to give us
 Something to live for here that shall outlive us?
  Some more substantial boon
Than such as flows and ebbs with Fortune's fickle moon?
  The little that we see
  From doubt is never free;
  The little that we do
  Is but half-nobly true;
  With our laborious hiving
 What men call treasure, and the gods call dross,
  Life seems a jest of Fate's contriving,
  Only secure in every one's conniving,
 A long account of nothings paid with loss."

But this is only the plaint of weariness,
the outcry of a spirit that is distressed by
the things that are seen, and that lacks the
vision of things unseen and eternal. And
the reassuring word can be no other than
that of the poet himself : —

 " But stay! no age was e'er degenerate,
  Unless men held it at too cheap a rate;
  For in our likeness still we shape our fate.

Ah, there is something here
Unfathomed by the cynic's sneer,
Something that gives our feeble light
A high immunity from Night,
Something that leaps life's narrow bars
To claim its birthright with the hosts of heaven;
A seed of sunshine that can leaven
Our earthly dulness with the beams of stars,
And glorify our clay
With light from fountains elder than the Day;
A conscience more divine than we,
A gladness fed with secret tears,
A vexing, forward-reaching sense
Of some more noble permanence;
A light across the sea,
Which haunts the soul and will not let it be,
Still beaconing from the heights of undegenerate years."

It is only as this inspiration of a sacred purpose, this sense of a holy obligation, comes to those who lead in the great affairs of state; only as the people themselves become aware of the truth that this nation, as truly as that other nation in the wilderness, needs the pillar of cloud by day and of fire by night, that light will break upon our future, and we shall behold with assured vision the calm peace for which we wait and pray.

It is not, then, solely or chiefly of our duty to Cæsar that we as American citizens are called to think, but of our duty as Cæsars, — kaisers, rulers of this free land. Who is Cæsar? Who is the king? He is the anointed of God. He is the one whom God has chosen and set apart to rule. Such anointing and consecration has every one of us received, into whose hand is put the ballot. It is not our power that we wield: we have no power; there is but one absolute Ruler, the Lord our righteousness. To us the power is intrusted by Him, that we may use it in his name. Let Cæsar render to God what belongs to Him.

VIII.

PUBLIC OPINION.

What I want to impress you with is the great weight that is attached to the opinion of everything that can call itself a man. Give me anything that walks erect and can read, and he shall count one in the millions of the Lord's sacramental host, which is yet to come up and trample all oppression in the dust. — WENDELL PHILLIPS, *Speeches*, First Series, page 50.

All free governments, whatever their name, are in reality governments by public opinion, and it is on the quality of this public opinion that their prosperity depends. It is, therefore, their first duty to purify the element from which they draw the breath of life. With the growth of democracy grows also the fear, if not the danger, that this atmosphere may be corrupted with poisonous exhalations from lower and more malarious levels, and the question of sanitation becomes more instant and pressing. Democracy, in its best sense, is merely the letting in of light and air. — JAMES RUSSELL LOWELL, *Democracy and Other Addresses*, page 38.

VIII.

PUBLIC OPINION.

ONE of the subjects concerning which a new conception of duty is greatly needed is the relation of the individual to the public opinion of the community. The creation and diffusion of a sound public opinion may be said to be the primary social duty. Public opinion is the motive power of democratic institutions. It bears the same relation to Christian society that protoplasm bears to life.

In that great treatise of Mr. James Bryce upon the American Commonwealth, one whole Part, twelve chapters, covering 122 closely-printed pages, is devoted to this subject of Public Opinion. It might be instructive to read the headings of these chapters: " The Nature of Public Opinion ; Government by Public Opinion ; How Pub-

lic Opinion Rules in America; Organs of
Public Opinion; National Characteristics
as Moulding Public Opinion; Classes as In-
fluencing Opinion; Local Types of Opinion
East, West, and South; The Action of
Public Opinion; The Fatalism of the Multitude; The Tyranny of the Majority;
Wherein Public Opinion Fails; Wherein
Public Opinion Succeeds." This will serve
to show what estimate is placed by a great
publicist upon this force as it affects our
social and national welfare.

Nearly all modern governments are governments by public opinion. The case has
greatly altered since the Oriental despot,
whose will was the only law, was the type
of the civil ruler. Louis XIV., a century
and a half ago, could say in France:
"What is the State? I am the State."
But it is long since anybody would dare to
say that in France. The Czar of Russia
comes pretty near being an absolute ruler,
but nothing is so clear as that his absolu-
tism is his weakness. The fiery young Ger-

man emperor talks large about " my government" and " my people," and assumes
that he alone is responsible for the conduct
of affairs in that great empire; nevertheless,
he is beginning to listen well to the under-
tone of public opinion.

"Opinion," says Mr. Bryce, "has really
been the chief and ultimate power in nearly
all nations at nearly all times. I do not
mean merely the opinion of the class to
which the rulers belong. Obviously, the
small oligarchy of Venice was influenced
by the opinion of the Venetian nobility, as
the absolute Czar is influenced now by the
opinion of his court and his army. I mean
the opinion, unspoken, unconscious, but not
the less real and potent, of the masses of the
people. Governments have always rested,
and, special cases apart, must rest, if not
on the affection, then on the reverence or
awe; if not on the active approval, then
on the silent acquiescence, of the numerical
majority. It is only by rare exception that
the monarch or an oligarchy has maintained

authority against the will of the people. . . . The difference between despotically governed and free countries does not consist in the fact that the latter are ruled by opinion and the former by force, for both are generally ruled by opinion. It consists rather in this, that in the former the people instinctively obey a power which they do not know to be really of their own creation and to stand by their own permission ; whereas in the latter the people feel their supremacy, and consciously treat their rulers as their agents, while the rulers obey a power which they admit to have made and to be able to unmake them, — the popular will." [1]

When our Declaration of Independence says that rulers derive all their *just* powers from the consent of the governed, we may question the form of the apothegm. If it means that the consent of the governed makes the rule just, we must dissent. Rulers may obtain the consent of the governed to do an unjust thing ; their consent does

---

[1] *The American Commonwealth*, ii. 216–219.

not make it just. A majority vote for a wrong does not make it right. The quality of justice is not given to the act of a magistrate by the approval of the people; that quality is tested by other standards. The magistrate's act may be just, though all the people disapprove; it may be unjust, though they unanimously approve. This is not likely, but it is possible.

But though justice is not due to popular consent, power is; we may truly say that governments derive their *effective* powers from the consent of the people; to be *efficient*, the government must follow the general direction of public opinion.

Legislation is, in a general way, the crystallization into statutes of public opinion. It is not always so, indeed; sometimes a few men get notions into their heads which they conceive to be expedient or beneficial, and succeed, by adroitly manipulating legislative bodies, in getting them framed into law, although they do not represent the wishes or the judgment of any considerable number of the people. Such legislation is generally nugatory; and a great mass of dead laws, which have had some such origin, incumber our statute - books. Living and effective laws are, however, the expression of public opinion; they put into legal form what the majority of the people have been thinking and wishing.

It is public opinion, also, that makes the executive strong, and that gives vigor and force to the administration of the laws. If the mayor or the sheriff or the state executive knows that the people demand the enforcement of any given law, he is likely to enforce it diligently. He may, from interested motives, be remiss or negligent, but he is not likely to be; he does not think it safe; he feels the pressure of public opinion, and yields to it. If, on the other hand, there be any law whose execution depends on the will of the magistrate, and concerning which the people have ceased to have a positive opinion and an active interest, its enforcement is apt to be lax. There are exceptional cases in which this is not true. There are magistrates who, when intrusted with the enforcement of law, regard themselves as bound to do the thing that they have sworn to do, whether the pressure of public opinion is felt or not. They assume that public opinion has already expressed itself in the enactment of the law; that the people in electing them must be understood as commanding them to execute the law; and that they have no right to sit down and wait until public opinion prompts and impels and scourges them to action. This, I think, is the only right and sound theory of the function of an executive; but, unfortunately, there are a good many executives who do not think so; who will do about what they are driven to do by the immediate pressure of public opinion, and not much more.

In view of this fact, it behooves the people, who are the rulers, to do one of two things, — either to elect men who will observe their oaths and execute the laws, without being prompted and prodded by public opinion ; or else to create and maintain an active public opinion, by which derelict officials shall be prompted and prodded to do their duty. And perhaps the safest course would be to do both these things at once.

If, then, public opinion not only makes but executes our laws, its vast importance in our social and national life must be evident. It is, indeed, the power that rules the republic. It is the force which drives all our governmental machinery. It is a little more than power, it is direction, also. It not only makes the machinery go, it determines the course that it shall take, the product that it shall evolve. The steam that drives the engine of the ship does not guide the vessel, it simply produces motion ; the hand of the helmsman determines the direction of the vessel. The steam that sets the spindles and the looms and the lathes in motion does not determine what the machinery shall produce. But public opinion, by its very nature, is directive as well as impulsive; it sets the machinery of government in motion, and tells it what to do; it moves the propeller, and it also holds the helm.

It is, then, of the very deepest importance that it should be sound and strong, with plenty of push and propulsion in it, and that it should also be sane and wise, so that the movements which it causes shall be guided to right ends.

I have already intimated that it is by no means infallible. It is the power that rules the republic; and the governmental defects and failures of the republic are due, in the final analysis, to the infirmity or the perversion or the misdirection of this power.

Public opinion may be weak. There may be a lack of general and active interest in public questions. Everybody may be so busy with his own personal and private affairs that he shall have no time or thought left for public affairs, or, if he thinks of them at all, thinks of them only as they affect his private interests. In such a case, we have nothing that can properly be termed public opinion ; we have a great mass of conflicting and quarreling private wishes and aims, but no real concern for the common weal. I fear that this is a condition to which, in our eager, money-making age, we sometimes approximate. We are so engrossed with our own enterprises and ambitions that we do not devote much serious time and thought to the concerns of the public. It is true that our private interests are often greatly affected by public action. When the city government becomes reckless and corrupt, and taxes grow to be enormous, we feel the burden keenly, and are ready to contribute to the formation of public opinion a good deal of energetic grumbling. When the tariff affects our business, we feel constrained to take a hand in discussing it, albeit we may not be able to tell very definitely what is wrong and how to right it. But this kind of opinion, which springs solely from a regard for our own selfish interests, is not the kind of public opinion which ought to rule the republic. Doubtless there does often come out of this struggle of conflicting interests a resultant force, by which the action of the legislatures and the magistrates is swayed; but this is not what we mean by a sound and strong public opinion.

It is generally true of our people, however, that there is, apart from this desire to secure such public action as shall advance our private interests, a good deal of thought and care among us, directed to the public welfare. We are not, as a people, destitute of the instincts and impulses of patriotism. The national or the municipal weal is often in our mind, and we desire to do what we can to promote it. I would not say that public opinion is a weak or ineffective force in this country; I often wish that it were stronger; but it is sometimes very powerful.

But public opinion needs to be sane and wise as well as strong. It ought to guide as well as propel. It needs not only muscles to push, but eyes to see. It is here that

its worst failures appear.   What we call
public opinion — that is, the popular impulse and demand — is often horribly blind,
fickle, cruel.   One day Public Opinion met
the Man of Nazareth, entering the city of
Jerusalem, and strewed his path with gar-
ments and palm - branches, shouting "Ho-
sanna to the Son of David!   Blessed is He
that cometh in the name of the Lord!"
Five days later, this same Public Opinion
found utterance through a raging mob, that
stormed at the door of Pilate's judgment
hall, and shouted, "Not this man, but Ba-
rabbas!   Away with this man!   Crucify
him!   crucify him!"   Public opinion
crowded the Duomo in Florence with ap-
plauding audiences when Savonarola spoke
from its pulpit in March, and in April it
sacked his convent and clamored for his
blood.   Public opinion swept this country
with one political verdict in the autumn of
1892, and with what was understood to be a
directly contradictory verdict in the autumn
of 1893.   I do not think that either action

was guided by reason. It was a matter of impulse and prejudice more than of judgment.

Indeed, so long as the majority of individuals are controlled in their conduct more by prejudice and impulse than by reason and judgment, we must expect that what we call public opinion will be largely swayed by gusts of passion, by tidal waves of reasonless infatuation and blind antipathy. And the truth is, that an aggregation of prejudiced and passionate men is far more irrational than any one of them. A mob is more brainless and more cruel than any single man of the mob would be likely to be if he were acting independently. I have seen the mob spirit take possession of an ecclesiastical assembly, prejudice and passion usurping the place of reason and conscience; and I have seen very unjust and cruel deeds done under that inspiration.

It is evident, then, that the force which we describe as public opinion is not always wise when it is strong.   It is liable to make fatal mistakes and to do terrible mischiefs. And the real trouble with it, generally, is that it is not truly public *opinion*, but public prejudice and public passion.   If it were the aggregate *thought* of the whole multitude, it would be less likely to go astray ; but the concentrated *passion* of the multitude is not so safe a guide.   In a multitude of counselors there is sometimes wisdom ; but in a multitude of shouters there is only noise.   To infuse into this incoherent and tumultuous mass of sentiment and impulse a little more informing and guiding thought is, then, the first thing to be desired.

Such, then, is this force that shapes constitutions and statutes, that lifts up and casts down governors and magistrates.   It seems a very weak thing ; but when the breath of God is in it, it is mighty to the pulling down of strongholds ; and when the fumes of the pit pervade it, the commonwealth becomes pandemonium.   When public opinion is sound and wholesome, social evils go down before it, as the snow disappears under the May-day sun ; when public opinion is feeble and ineffectual, all manner of abuses come forth and intrench themselves in society and in government. And I say that the importance of creating and diffusing a sound public opinion is very little understood by most of us. Surely, this is the central and vital element in our national life. Public opinion means to the republic all that power means to machinery. Any man who is building a steamship or a factory thinks first about his power. It is useless and absurd to build engines or machines, no matter how perfect, unless there is power to run them. But we Americans give ten times as much thought, in our politics, to the construction of political machinery, as we do to the provision of adequate and well-directed power to move it. But public opinion is far more to the republic than power is to machinery. It is all that the life-blood in the veins is to the human body. It is the vital element of the national life. To keep it pure and healthy, and thoroughly vitalized with the living breath of God, is the most important task that any Christian patriot can place before his mind.

And how is it that right public opinion is created? The newspaper is supposed to have something to do with it; but there are two theories about the function of the newspaper. By some persons the newspaper is suppose to generate public opinion; by others merely to reflect it. The most conspicuous journal in the world, the " London Times," has been conducted on the theory that it is the business of the newspaper to understand and express public opinion. The other theory is the one most commonly held, — that a newspaper ought to instruct and guide public opinion. Practically, however, the tendencies just now are all in the other direction; for what is called journalism is more and more regarded as a business; and the commercial success of the venture is the first thing considered. When this is the case, the counting-room, of course, dictates the policy of the paper ; and this can mean nothing else than that the chief effort will be to conform to the prevailing public sentiment, and not to antagonize it. Doubtless much is done by the best newspapers to instruct and invigorate public opinion, and much is done by the worst to mislead and debauch it. I am by no means sure on which side is the preponderance. But I am very sure that it will never do to depend on that agency for the creation and maintenance of the kind of public opinion which will rule the state beneficently.

Really this task is a very simple one, so simple that we altogether overlook its importance. Public opinion is merely the aggregate opinion of all the people, the resultant movement of the various thought of many men with many minds. All that is needed for the formation of a sound public opinion is that the great majority of the people should have clear ideas on subjects of public concernment, and should freely

express them. Nothing can be simpler than
this solution ; but simple things are not always easy. The solution of the temperance
problem is simple, — get everybody to stop
drinking ; but it is not easy. Still it is well
to keep before us the fact that as the ocean
is made up of water-drops, so the power
which sways governments and works righteousness in the earth is only the combination of the thoughts and judgments of the
various individuals who compose the masses
of the people. And the sense of individual
responsibility for the invigoration and direction of the power needs to be cultivated by
every one of us. This is manifestly one of
the cases in which what is everybody's business may be nobody's. That maxim needs
to be supplanted by the sounder saying :
" What is everybody's business must be my
business."

The duty of the individual must involve
first, some careful effort to form opinions
upon questions of public welfare. What is
wanted is opinion, individual judgment,

upon all these questions. Mere impressions
or prepossessions are not sufficient; every
man ought to know what can be said against
the position he takes, as well as what can
be said for it; and his conclusion should
represent an honest attempt to bring the
question of the hour under the light of reason, and to find out all the facts upon which
a sound judgment should be based. It must
be admitted that, in spite of the free schools
of which we boast so much, the popular
ignorance upon vital questions of political
and social morality is still vast and profound, even here in republican America.
Witness the financial schemes of the most
transparent immorality and absurdity which
constantly flourish among us; witness, also,
the epidemics of brutal intolerance that oc-
casionally sweep over the land; and notice
how easy it is for political advocates to convince the masses that any lack of prosperity
must be the fault of the party in power.
Upon these larger questions of the state
there is, however, far more intelligence than

upon matters of local government. Very
few citizens take any pains to inform themselves respecting the administration of the
town or the city in which they live. They
take a great deal more interest in the tariff
debate or the Hawaiian imbroglio than in
the organized raids made upon the treasury
of their own town by the gang that always
beleaguers it, and in the offensive and de-
fensive alliances existing between their local
officials and the lawless classes. There is
often a great deal of vague suspicion and
accusation respecting all this; but of clear
and positive knowledge there is not much.
The citizens do not, as a rule, take pains to
inform themselves. Therefore there cannot
be any adequate force of public opinion to
deal with them. There is sometimes a good
deal of impatient and irritated feeling, but
it is apt to strike out wildly and attack the
wrong person, or make charges that cannot
be sustained. In order that no injustice
may be done, that the Demos may not degenerate into a mob and destroy the right-

eous with the wicked, there is need that the citizens should possess the intelligence from which may spring a rational public opinion.

Some sense of the importance of clear knowledge upon these great matters is evidently taking possession of the public mind. Within the past few years there has been a great revival of interest in social and civic problems; groups of men and women in almost every community are studying them with the most enthusiastic interest. In all the colleges and universities, questions of this class have suddenly been advanced to the forefront of the curriculum; the amount of work done upon subjects which relate to the public welfare is, I suppose, fourfold greater than it was twenty years ago. All this gives promise of a day when the first prerequisite of a sound public opinion — clear and accurate knowledge of public questions — shall be more fully supplied than it is at the present time.

But it is not enough to have clear ideas about public affairs; we must also be brave enough to utter them. The ignorance of the American citizen about the business affairs and the social conditions of his own municipality is often reprehensible, but his cowardice is far worse. That which he does know full well, he often will not declare. It will make him disagreeably prominent, perhaps; it will lead to discussions and controversies which it is pleasanter to avoid; it will bring down upon him the wrath of the classes who live by plunder; it will disturb some of his social relations; it may injure his business; therefore, he seals his lips and refuses to testify. How few men we find in any community, who have the courage of their convictions upon questions that concern the public welfare, — who are willing to speak right out in criticism of that which is palpably wrong. How many there are who are ready to say, when you appeal to them for support in any enterprise which involves conflict with evil powers: "I shall be glad to aid you financially, but it must be confidential; my name must not appear;

I cannot afford to have it known that I am identified with the scheme." Assistance of this sort is really worth very little. Many of our reforms have split upon this rock. What is most wanted is something that money cannot buy; it is precisely that which these crafty citizens withhold, — the personal influence and support of the reputable classes. If all the men who sit in their counting-rooms and write their checks in aid of good causes would come out into the public square and declare themselves the friends of these causes, there would be very little need of money; an invigorated public opinion would push the enterprise to its goal.

The utterance of the truth that is in him, bravely, clearly, constantly, upon all questions of public duty, — this is one of the primary obligations of every citizen of a republican state. The obligation of the Christian citizen is precisely the same as that of the Christian believer. Conviction is not enough; there must also be confession.

What the man believes in the heart he must declare with the lips. To be ashamed or afraid to utter the truth that he believes is the gravest of delinquencies. And there is just as much reason that the citizen should witness a good confession as there is that the disciple should do so. Indeed, the reasons are the same in both cases. The prevalence of the spiritual kingdom of our Lord is secured by faithful witnessing. It is by the testimony of believers that converts are made and the kingdom is extended and established. If every man who knows that Christ is king would speak out and tell what he knows, his kingdom would come with power. We may say that it is the divine plan that a sound and vigorous public opinion should be created in favor of the kingdom of heaven; and that it is to be created by the outspoken confession of loyalty on the part of individual believers. The same law holds in regard to the promotion of all social and civic reforms. These, too, depend upon the public opinion of the

community, and the public opinion of the
community is simply the consentaneous voice
of individual men and women openly declar-
ing the truth that is in their minds. Such
utterance sometimes costs discomfort and
suffering; but let no man suppose that civic
righteousness and social peace can be won
without sacrifice. It cost something to establish our liberties; it costs something to
preserve them, — more, I fear, than some of
us are willing to pay. But the beginning
of all good fidelity to the trust committed to
us is here, — in the willingness to know the
truth respecting the interests committed to
our charge, and in the readiness to speak
the truth we know without fear or favor, on
every proper occasion, whether men will
hear or whether they will forbear. It is the
most elementary of all our public obligations; it is also, I think, the most stringent.
Infidelity to this obligation produces a social
malady for which there is no cure; fidelity
to this obligation creates a social force in
whose presence no evil can long endure.

IX.

PHARISAISM.

Look at the character in its essence, only changing its dress, its class of particular virtues, according to circumstances, and taking off one and putting on another as the public standard shifts; thus cleared of its accidents, look at it; is there anything old about it? It is new; it is fresh; it is modern; it is living; it is old in the sense of human nature being old, but in no other. It is a type of evil much more likely to increase than decay, — to increase as the standard of advancing society throws the corrupt principle in man more upon policy rather than open heathen resistance. Formality and routine are not essential to the Pharisee; he feeds his character upon ancient disciplinarian virtues, if he has nothing else to feed it upon; but he flourishes quite as much upon utilitarian and active virtues if they are uppermost. — J. B. MOZLEY, *University and Other Sermons*, page 39.

He condemned equally the conduct of the Pharisees and their perversions of the law, and found in their unveracious dealing with the Scriptures the secret and explanation of all their other unveracities. Their traditions transgressed the commandments of God. . . . The most absolute slave of the letter is always the man who does it most violence. While he professes to be devoted to the law, he devises interpretations that annul its most distinctive precepts. — A. M. FAIRBAIRN, *Studies in the Life of Christ*, page 171.

Some great pervasive and consolidated wrong may rest in the presence of the church, with hardly a perceptible power of rebuke on the part of the pulpit. . . . The church has no purchase, no leverage against it. It nourishes pietism, but loses humanity. — JOHN BASCOM, *The New Theology*, page 180.

PHARISAISM.

Is any new conception needed respecting Pharisaism? Nineteen hundred years ago it was a burning question: no issue was more vital or more deadly than that which it presented; the kingdom of heaven had no force to reckon with that was of greater importance. Is it a living issue? Is there anything in the world to-day resembling that dead wall of formalism and hypocrisy, which stood across the path of Him who came bringing life and immortality to light? Is Pharisaism an archæological curiosity or an ever-present fact? A little study may throw light upon these questions.

The Pharisees arose, as a party in the Jewish nation, a little more than a century and a half before the birth of Christ, under the reign of the Syrian dynasty.

After the exile, Judea was for some time a dependency of the Persian kingdom; sometimes there was a political representative of the Persian throne at Jerusalem, but a considerable degree of home rule was allowed, and the high priest was the real head of the nation. Thus the religious independence of the people was recognized, while they were politically subject to Persia. When Alexander the Great conquered Persia, Judea passed under the control of the Macedonian kings of Egypt; and then, still later, into the hands of the Greek rulers of Syria, the Seleucidæ. Under both these dynasties the religious liberty of the Jews was recognized, except during the reign of Antiochus Epiphanes, when a most determined attempt was made to stamp out the national faith and substitute for it the Greek Paganism. This attempt led to that patriotic rebellion of the Hasmoneans, or Maccabees, the last effort of the Jews to establish their independence. During this struggle the Pharisees arose. They were

not, strictly, a patriotic party; with the
aims of the Maccabean leaders to establish a Jewish dynasty they had not much
sympathy. If Judea became politically independent, the state would exercise considerable control over the church; politics and
religion would, in their judgment, be too
much mixed. Indeed, some of these Maccabean rulers had assumed the office of high
priest, and had exercised its functions. This
was wholly contrary to the ideas of the
Pharisees. They wished to keep religion
and politics entirely separate. They cared
very little for political independence; they
preferred that the nation should have a foreign master, who would leave them free to
develop their religious life in their own way.
The Sadducees were the party that sup-
ported the efforts of the Hasmoneans for political independence; but the Pharisees, like
a good many people in these days, thought
that the sacred and the secular should be
kept entirely distinct. " The Hasmoneans,"
says Wellhausen, " had no hereditary right

to the high-priesthood, and their politics, which aimed at the establishment of a national monarchy, were contrary to the whole spirit and essence of the second theocracy. The presupposition of that theocracy was foreign domination; in no other way could its sacred, *i. e.* clerical, character be maintained. God and the law could not but be forced into the background, if a warlike kingdom, retaining indeed the forms of a hierocracy, but really violating its spirit at every point, should ever grow out of a mere pious community. Above all, how could the scribes hope to retain their importance, if temple and synagogue were cast into the shade by politics and clash of arms."[1] In the early years of the Maccabean insurrection the patriotic spirit of the Jews triumphed over the Pharisaic spirit, and the influence of this party was very slight. But gradually their numbers increased, and their power strengthened, until, in the time of Christ, they were the predominant party;

[1] *Encyclopædia Britannica*, article " Israel."

the Scribes and the Pharisees, as the gospel records make plain, were the ruling faction when our Lord was on the earth.

The very fact that the religious ideas of the Pharisees constrained them to take an unpatriotic attitude, and to look with disfavor upon attempts to restore the national independence, would raise in some minds a question as to the genuineness of their religion. A faith that is at war with patriotism needs, at any rate, to be scrutinized. Such was not the faith of the early prophets; and in all the later centuries, love of God and love of country have finely blended in the characters of the noblest of earth.

No complete statement of the peculiar tenets of the Pharisees can here be given: a few illustrative particulars must suffice.

The Pharisees were the people of the Law. To them the Torah, the Mosaic legislation, embodied the sum of all wisdom. Every dot and every curve of every letter of that law was significant. And besides this, they held that the written law had been accompanied by an oral law, explaining and expanding it; which oral law had been handed down by tradition, and was every whit as sacred and binding as the text of the Mosaic books. The worship of the letter, to which the Pharisees thus became devoted, was the most elaborate system of externalism ever invented. Every religious observance was hedged about with the most minute and fantastic directions and explanations; so that if the rite had originally possessed some spiritual significance, its meaning would be completely buried out of sight beneath the superincumbent mass of rubric. Thus, to give only a single example, it was supposed to be the duty of every Jew to light candles in his house on the eve of the Sabbath. It is not clear whence this observance arose, for there is no Levitical rule requiring it. But it had been accepted as part of the regular programme, and then the doctors began to speculate as to how these candles should be lighted. One would have said that the mere method of lighting them could not be of any great consequence, if only their cheerful light appeared in the home; but the one who said that could not have been a Pharisee. To him this was a very profound and important question, far more serious than any inquiry that could possibly arise concerning your duty to your neighbor. And this was part of his reasoning about it, as extracted from a Jewish prayer book: "With what sort of wick and oil are the candles of the Sabbath to be lighted, and with what are they not to be lighted? They are not to be lighted with the woolly substance that grows upon cedars, nor with undressed flax, nor with silk, nor with rushes, nor with leaves out of the wilderness, nor with moss that grows on the surface of water, nor with pitch, nor with wax, nor with oil made of cotton-seed, nor with the fat of the tail or the entrails of beasts. Nathan Hamody saith it may be lighted with boiled suet; but the wise men say, be it boiled or not boiled, it may not be lighted with it.

It may not be lighted with burnt oil on festival days. Rabbi Ishmael says it may not be lighted with train-oil, because of honor to the Sabbath; but the wise men allow all sorts of oil; with mixed oil, oil of nuts, oil of radish seed, oil of fish, of gourd seed, of resin and gum. Rabbi Tarphun saith they are not to be lighted but with oil of olives. Nothing that grows out of the woods is used for lighting but flax, and nothing that grows out of woods doth pollute by the pollution of a tent but flax; the wick of cloth that is doubled, and hath not been singed, Rabbi Eleazar saith it is unclean and may not be lighted withal; Rabbi Akibah says it is clean and may be lighted withal. A man may not split a shell of an egg and fill it with oil and put it in the socket of a candlestick, because it shall blaze, though the candlestick be of earthenware; but Rabbi Jehudah permits it; if the potter made it with a hole through at first, it is allowed because it is the same vessel. No man shall fill a platter with oil and give it place next to the lamp and put the head of a wick on a platter to make it drop the oil; but Rabbi Jehudah permits it." [1]

Does this convey a precise idea to any mind respecting what may and may not be done in this extremely critical matter of lighting the candles at home on the Sabbath eve? Would a conscientious Jew, anxious to fulfill the law to the very letter, be perfectly clear as to his duty, after he had waded through these voluminous directions? I should think that early candle-lighting on the eve of the Sabbath, in a Jewish household, must have been a time of great solicitude. What our Lord says about the manner in which the Scribes and Pharisees made the law void by their traditions, and about their binding heavy burdens and grievous to be borne and laying them on men's shoulders, finds some explanation in these extracts from their own literature.

Pharisaism was the deification of detail, the apotheosis of the trivial. It put so

[1] Smith's *Bible Dictionary*, article "Pharisees."

much stress upon minutiæ that no weight was left for things momentous. In leveling up petty technicalities it leveled down great principles. If you undertake, in reading the Constitution of the United States, to ascribe deep and profound significance to the dot over every *i* and the tail of every comma, dwelling, for hours at a time, on such trivialities, it is clear that you will never comprehend the real meaning of that instrument. And the mind that is trained to weigh and measure and discuss these ridiculous trifles utterly loses its grasp upon the serious things of life.

The inevitable effect of this exaltation of insignificant things is thus a woeful lack of moral perspective. Religious routine is the main thing; the great values of character, the great claims of humanity, take a subordinate place. Mint and anise and cummin are to be tithed with religious scrupulosity, but judgment, mercy, and faith go by default. "In the hearing of all the people," we are told, Jesus "said unto his disciples,

Beware of the Scribes, which desire to walk in long robes, and love salutations in the market-places, and chief seats in the synagogues, and chief places at feasts; which devour widows' houses, and for a pretense make long prayers : these shall receive greater condemnation." The denunciations which Jesus visited upon these people are terrible ; the words flash and crackle to this day with the intensity of indignation : " Woe unto you, Scribes and Pharisees, hypocrites! for ye build the sepulchres of the prophets and garnish the tombs of the righteous, and say, If we had been in the days of our fathers, we should not have been partakers with them in the blood of the prophets. Wherefore ye witness to yourselves that ye are sons of them that slew the prophets. Fill ye up then the measure of your fathers. Ye serpents, ye offspring of vipers, how shall ye escape the judgment of hell?" " It is difficult," says one, " to avoid the conclusion that his repeated denunciations of the Pharisees mainly exasperated them into taking measures for causing his death; so that in one sense He may be said to have shed his blood and to have laid down his life in protesting against their practice and spirit. . . . Hence, to understand the Pharisees is, by contrast, an aid towards understanding the spirit of uncorrupted Christianity."

The absolute contrast between the spirit of Christianity and the spirit of Pharisaism it is hardly necessary to point out. Pharisaism puts its emphasis upon externals, Christianity upon the spirit and the life; Pharisaism is a system of minute rules, Christianity rests upon great principles; Pharisaism cares most for the perfection of ritual and least for the perfection of character; Christianity regards as hateful and accursed any mere formality which is put forward as a screen for evil conduct. The men who devour widows' houses and for a pretense make long prayers are the men on whom falls the withering malediction of the meek and lowly Jesus.

It would seem that the evil thing against

which our Lord waged such relentless warfare, and which, at the last, was his mur-
derer, could never find entrance into his
church; and yet it must be owned that
much of the leaven of the Pharisees is mixed
with our modern Christianity. We cannot
conceive that Jesus could maintain any other
attitude before it than that which He held
nineteen centuries ago; and we must won-
der what He would say if He entered some
modern churches and found the essential
spirit of Pharisaism comfortably installed
behind their altars.

The manifestations of this spirit are
many. The exaltation of details and technicalities to the great neglect of the everlasting verities is a type of Pharisaism
which is common enough: how often do we
find the servants of Christ chaffering and
quarreling about some petty question of
dogma or ritual, which has not the slightest
bearing upon character, while the great concerns of the kingdom of heaven are utterly
neglected. The questions about which the

sects differ are mostly questions of this character. They themselves are swift witnesses to the truth of this statement, for each of them is always making haste to declare that Christians of other names are all traveling in the same road and going to the same place. But what an infinite amount of fussing and puttering there is about these petty distinctions, which are not differences. Cannot these stalwart sectarians see that it is the leaven of the Pharisees that is working in all these foolish fermentations ?

But the type of modern Pharisaism to which I wish chiefly to draw attention is of a much more dangerous description. It is that which grows out of the tendency to identify the religious life with certain set practices and observances, and to feel that one who is punctual in these is to be esteemed a saint, no matter what his real character may be. There are many good people among us who put so much emphasis upon the mere going through the motions of the worshiper and devotee, that they are unable to take much interest in matters of every-day behavior.

Another element sometimes complicates problems of this nature. If the man who is punctual in all the customary observances is also a liberal giver to churches and benevolent causes, the case is practically closed in many minds. Such a man must be a good man. To question it is next door to blasphemy.

I heard a good clergyman talking, not long ago, about a public character, whose conduct, as I happened to have abundant evidence, has been most perfidious, — a man whose greed has made him unscrupulous in pushing his fortunes; who has trampled upon equity and justice and honor and all the rights of his neighbors. Of him the good clergyman warmly said: " Why, here is this man, against whom such horrible charges are made, and what do you think? I found out the other day that this man is a devoted Christian ; he always goes to church, and to prayer-meeting; he has family prayers, and he asks a blessing at the table at every meal." That, in the clergyman's judgment, seemed to be conclusive evidence that the accused person was a good man, — anybody who did all those pious things must be a good man. He did not say that the extortions and crimes of which the other was charged were all balanced and offset by this fidelity to the minor religious obligations; of course, he would not say just that: but it was evident that, in view of this man's exemplary observances, the clergyman's mind was practically sealed against any evidence that could incriminate him. And this was because, all unconsciously, no doubt, he had come to put so much weight on mere observances that the great tests of character were obscured.

"There is another man," the clergyman went on, "about whom stories of the same kind have been told. But this man, as I have been told, has built an elegant church and parsonage, and has presented it to the Presbyterian society with which he worships." "But suppose," said a listener, "that those train robbers who, after murdering the express messenger not far from here the other night, secured one hundred thousand dollars, had come to you, red-handed from their raid, and had offered you ten thousand dollars for your church, would you have given them a certificate of Christian character?" The question would have been impertinent if it had not been pertinent. But what shall we say of the state of mind which can parry grave and well-founded charges of moral delinquency with assertions of pietistic virtue and with testimonies concerning gifts to churches? Is there not great danger, in many quarters, of putting much more stress upon these practices than upon doing justly, loving mercy, and walking humbly before God?

There is reason to fear that a good many of us clergymen are quite too much disposed to make men very comfortable who punctually go through with the motions of religion, especially if they are liberal contributors.

The state of mind is illustrated by the reply
of that good pastor who was asked by a notoriously wicked but wealthy man, whether
a liberal gift of money to the church would
improve his chances of heaven. The good
clergyman scratched his head for a moment,
when a bright thought struck him : "It's
worth trying," he said. The shrewd humor
of the parson must not obscure the fact that
his policy is rather too common. The man
who will give to churches or colleges or theological seminaries large sums of money is
likely to get a great deal of notice and of
praise, even if his wealth has been gained
by methods utterly nefarious.

A few years ago, a religious newspaper,
with great boldness, attacked certain representatives of a strong commercial institution, accusing them of having not only
overpowered their rivals by utter unscrupulousness, but also of having tampered with
legislatures and courts. Another newspaper
of the same denomination replied to this with
much warmth. Did it undertake to disprove

the accusation? No; that could not be done. But it pronounced these men " Christian men of the highest excellence of character," declared that they were " eminent " members of its denomination, and that they " honored their religious obligations and contributed without stint to the noblest Christian and philanthropic objects." In view of this fact, any mere unscrupulousness in business, or any trifling attempts to corrupt courts or legislatures, or to aggrandize themselves by perjury or violence, were not, of course, to be spoken of. The other journal refused to be extinguished by this retort, and went on to quote Milton's answer to the similar plea made for King Charles : " For his private virtues they are beside the question. If he oppress and extort all day, shall he be held blameless because he prayeth at night and morning? "

This is a question upon which, as it seems to me, there is need of much searching of heart on the part of ministers of churches and presidents of colleges and theological seminaries, and indeed on the part of the community at large. The disposition is strong in many quarters to condone the most monstrous iniquities, — iniquities that strike at the vitals of the nation, — if the men who commit them will put on a cloak of religious observance, especially if the cloak has good capacious pockets, out of which liberal donations of hush-money are handed over now and then. Men who would certainly be in the penitentiary if they had their deserts are flattered and petted by the heads of great educational and religious institutions, and made to feel that they are regarded as the salt of the earth.

Is a church really benefited with money that it gets in this way, by confounding moral distinctions, and giving to great malefactors the honor that is due only to the upright? Is a college better equipped for its proper work with endowments which it secures by paying honor to pirates? I must be permitted to doubt it. And it seems to me that a college president who had the courage to say to any man who offered him large money which had been notoriously gotten by fraud and rapine: "Certainly, we will take your money, if you choose to give it to us; but you must give it with the distinct understanding that we shall teach our young men that it is a shameful thing to get wealth in the way that you have gotten yours, and that giving a part of it away in charity does not take off the curse," — any college president, I say, who was brave enough to say this, and stand by it, would earn for his college an endowment in Christian manliness worth far more to it than the tainted millions which it failed to gain.

What must be the effect upon young men in college of a policy displayed before them in the administration of the college, which exalts and honors rich plunderers for the sake of getting some of their booty? Are not young men educated by such spectacles in a more subtle and effective manner than by any sermons that are preached to them, or any instruction in theoretical ethics that they receive? Is it not these things that fix their standards and form their ideals? And are they well educated under such influences? Would they not be better educated in an institution with fewer laboratories, smaller libraries, homelier halls, wherein the modern Pharisee, who devours widows' houses, and for a pretense makes long prayers, is treated as Christ treated his tribe, no matter how princely his donations to learning and to charity?

For it is not difficult to discern that this type, which is all too common amongst us, is essentially Pharisaic. If the Lord, whom in our prayers we seek, should suddenly come to his temple, these are the men upon whom would fall his withering curse, — the men who by greed and extortion and injustice have heaped to themselves great riches, and are using some small portions of them to purchase for themselves the flattery of those who instruct our youth, and the adulation of those who minister at our altars.

And if those to whom this insincere hom-

age is paid are Pharisees, what shall we say
of those who bestow it? It is natural that
the malefactor should be willing to bribe the
witnesses for God to be silent concerning
his crimes, and to give him honor and distinction instead of the shame and ignominy
which are his due; but how about the men
who take the bribe? Must there not be a
terrible lack of moral perspective in the mind
that can condone great crimes because the
criminal goes through with the motions of
piety, and is ready to bestow in charity a
portion of his plunder? What has caused
this lack of moral perspective? It is the
fruit of a kind of religionism which puts
emphasis on trifles and slurs over the eternal verities: which tithes mint, anise, and
cummin, and neglects judgment, mercy, and
faith. Clearly, there is need, even yet, of
the great Master's warning: " Beware of the
leaven of the Pharisees."

X.

ONE BUT TWAIN.

Polarity, or action and reaction, we meet in every part of nature : in darkness and light ; in heat and cold ; in the ebb and flow of waters · in male and female ; in the inspiration and expiration of plants and animals ; in the equation of quantity and quality in the fluids of the human body ; in the systole and diastole of the heart ; in the undulations of fluids and of sound ; in the centrifugal and centripetal gravity ; in electricity, galvanism, and chemical affinity. Superinduce magnetism at one end of a needle : the opposite magnetism takes place at the other end. — RALPH WALDO EMERSON, *Essay on Compensation.*

The system of nature is a balance of antagonistic forces. This relation of the forces is not a restful equilibrium, but a fluctuating and compensating one, like that of the wave-rocked sea. It is an equilibrium of action and reaction which, in their more complicated forms, become great cycles of movement, coextensive with the entire field of nature and history. . . . At the bottom of the mental scale there is reflex action, and at the top mental action is counteraction. There is no mental conception of properties except by contrast ; one feeling antagonizes another ; the mind is itself a system of balances, often fluctuating from one extreme to another, and the will is forever the theatre of emotional conflict. And all this antagonism is not incidental and transitory as usually supposed, but fundamental and ineradicable. — *Reforms : Their Difficulties and Possibilities,* page 1.

X.

ONE BUT TWAIN.

THE progress of the kingdom of God is always obstructed by an irrational partisanship. The partisan is a man who can see but one side of a question. Now a great many questions have two sides, on each of which a great deal may be said. Human experience largely proceeds under a law of antagonism. Life in its end is not twain but one ; yet in its process, its development, it is often not one but twain.

We find here a great central law or principle of life, one that we must constantly keep in view in our studies and our conduct. The clear recognition of this law would cure at once the greater part of the reasonless partisanship now existing in the world. No more fruitful conception could be introduced into the mind of the average American

Christian than this conception of the dualism or two-sidedness of human experience,
of the fact that life is not one homogeneous
whole, but two distinct and dissimilar but
coördinate halves ; a sphere indeed, but two
hemispheres ; that its right action is a compound or resultant of two forces, which,
though not antagonistic in the sense of being exclusive or hostile, are yet opposed, as
the thumb is opposed to the fingers, as the
two blades of a pair of shears are opposed
to each other ; so that each is the comple-
ment of the other, and serves its purpose
by counteracting the other ; each being the
fulcrum, so to speak, on which the power
of the other rests ; neither being able to act
without the resistance of the other.

" An inevitable dualism," says Emerson,
" bisects nature, so that each thing is a half,
and suggests another thing to make it whole ;
as, spirit, matter ; man, woman ; odd, even ;
subjective, objective ; in, out ; upper, under ;
motion, rest ; yea, nay."

Something of this duplex character of

human life is suggested to us in the fact that our senses and faculties seem to be put up in pairs: we have two eyes, two ears, two nostrils, two hands, two feet; the brain itself has two distinctly divided lobes; every man has two sides or hemispheres of physical life and motion, the one of which may be helpless while the other is still active. The motive-power of a man is similar to that of a twin-screw steamer with two engines, one on either side the keel. And while it is true of the organs of sense that those on one side of the body may act without the coöperation of those on the other side, yet it is evident that the perfect action of either requires the action of the other; while many of the motions of the hands, like the motion of the thumb and the fingers, are in opposite directions; the power to grasp and hold large objects depends on this opposition and mutual resistance of the two hands.

Not only do we find this duplex arrangement of the organs and parts of the human body, we discover also the tremendous fact

of sex, which characterizes all the higher orders of organic existences, both plants and
animals. What the story of Genesis says
of man is true of many others of his fellow-
creatures, those that possess sensibility and
those that do not. " He made them in the
beginning, male and female." Neither sex,
alone, constitutes the unit of its species ;
the man is not " the one," as the querulous
wife complained, nor is the woman the one ;
the twain are one. The man is a fraction,
often a very vulgar and improper fraction
indeed, without the woman ; and the woman
without the man is not of much more account. And it is the merest commonplace
that the sexes are not duplicate but contrasted types; that each is a foil to the
other ; that by dissimilar physical, mental,
moral characteristics they react upon each
other both for stimulus and for restraint.
The average man's view of any question is
not the true view, nor is the average woman's ; by mutual criticism and correction
they reach the true view. The man's way

needs always to be modified by consideration and comparison of the woman's way.
In philosophy, religion, science, education,
economics, politics, we need and must have
the combined wisdom of both sexes. Man's
logic must be matched with woman's intui-
tion ; man's force with woman's gentleness.

This glimpse at the duplex character
of the human organism, and at the still
more marvelous division of the race into
two contrasted but harmonious halves, each
of which is indispensable to the welfare and
even to the existence of the other, may stimulate our search for a great law of nature,
to which the phenomena we are studying
will be found to conform. And we shall
not search in vain. At the very outset we
are confronted by the two great forces by
which the movements of the solar system are
controlled : the centrifugal force, by which
the planets are driven forward in right lines ;
and the centripetal force, by which they are
drawn directly toward the sun. It is the
marvelous combination and the perfect ad-

justment of these two forces that keeps the
planets moving in their elliptical orbits
round the sun. If either of them should
be canceled, or seriously weakened, the result would be chaos. It is to the perfect
equilibrium of these two forces, acting at
right angles to each other, that the order
of the planetary system is due.

And when we come to study more nar-
rowly the constitution of matter itself, we
find that the forces which make it at once
coherent and tractable are opposing forces.
The attraction that binds the atoms together
is matched by the repulsion that drives them
asunder. If there were no force but attraction, all matter would be not only solid but
rigid, inflexible, adamantine; there would
be no such process as decomposition or com-
bustion; there would be no air to breathe;
life would be impossible. If, on the other
hand, there were no force but repulsion, all
nature would be resolved at once into the
elemental gases. The combination of these
two opposing forces, attraction and repul-

sion, tension and pressure, results in the existing conditions of matter, with all its varied, manifold, changeful phenomena. If we find at the very heart of matter such a duality of powers, not one single, imperious, irresistible force, but two evenly matched forces standing over against each other, holding each other in check, and giving us in their equilibrium the very conditions of life, we need not be surprised to find that life and growth and progress are generally conformed to some such law.

If the material world exists in its present form as the result of the balancing of two great opposing energies, then it may be that the material world itself is only one member of a grander duality ; that mind and matter, the spiritual and the physical realms, stand correlated in the same way, acting and reacting upon each other, and giving us, in their mysterious conjunction, the phenomena of conscious life. There are philosophers who resolve all existence into mind ; who say that the phenomena of sense are only illusions; that what appear to us to be the qualities of matter are only the reflections of our own consciousness. On the other side, there are philosophers who resolve all existence into matter; who affirm that our mental operations are only refinements of physical force; that man has no separate spiritual existence; that the soul is the brain; that thought is only a subtle property of matter. These two schools of thought have been contending for the field, with various fortunes, since the birth of philosophy. The extreme idealists say there is no matter, no external world that we can know anything about; the materialists say that there is no mind, no spiritual world of which we have any knowledge whatever. The tendency of human nature is to take the one side or the other of this dispute. Philosophers seem to think that it simplifies nature if you can bring all its phenomena under one law. So it does; but perhaps the important thing is not to simplify nature, but to tell the truth about it. It often simplifies a complicated story to leave about half of the truth untold. It often simplifies a difficult problem to ignore a moiety of the facts. But those truths untold, those facts ignored, are sure to come back and plague you. The idealist thinks that his theory of the universe is much more intelligible if he resolves all the phenomena of sensation into mental processes ; and the materialist thinks that he gets rid of many mental and moral difficulties by denying the separate existence of the soul. But each must practically assume the existence of the facts that he logically denies, or he will behave in the one case like a lunatic, and in the other like a knave.

It would seem, then, that experience vindicates an interpretation of the universe which recognizes the existence of both mind and matter, of the spiritual as well as of the material realm, and seeks to define their relation. That is often a very difficult task ; the border-lands in which mind and matter come together are regions of great obscurity; it is often difficult to draw the line between the two realms; they shade into each other by degrees that are absolutely imperceptible by any powers that we possess; nevertheless, the boundary is there, and omniscience can trace it. There is a realm of spiritual powers, and there is a realm of material forces, and the phenomena of intelligent and conscious life lie partly in the one realm and partly in the other. Man is a spirit, and man has a body; the body is as real as the spirit, and the spirit is as real as the body. Every man is the incarnation of a spiritual existence in a material form. The relation of these two he can never fully understand; there are mysteries here which no insight can penetrate, no dialectics dissolve; but the fact is clear enough to most people of common sense. Neither side of this dual personality is to be ignored or despised; the hands must minister to the needs of the spirit; the conscience and the love must rule and transfigure the functions of the body. A man's religion must permeate

his earthly affairs, and his humanity must
vitalize his faith.

> " For pleasant is this flesh;
>   Our soul, in its rose-mesh
> Pulled ever to the earth, still yearns for rest;
>   Would we some prize might hold
>   To match those manifold
> Possessions of the brute, — gain most, as we did best!

> " Let us not always say,
>   'Spite of this flesh to-day
> I strove, made head, gained ground upon the whole!'
>   As the bird wings and sings,
>   Let us cry, ' All good things
> Are ours, nor soul helps flesh more, now, than flesh helps
>   soul!' "

We find these balancings of diverse or
opposing tendencies in every department of
thought and life.   Not only in the elements
and factors of existence, but in the social
forces, this law is discovered.   It is a very
old remark that harmonious and healthful
social conditions are the result of the combination of two opposing tendencies, — the
disposition to make changes, and the disposition to resist changes.   A society in which

there are no conservatives has no stability, and a society in which there are no liberals has no movement. The determination to preserve the *status quo*, and the determination to revolutionize the *status quo*, are always present in the most vigorous communities; and the welfare of the state depends on their being pretty fairly balanced. The conservatives always contemn the radicals, and count them the enemies of the commonwealth; and the radicals always hate the conservatives, and deem them the foes of progress; but each is the proper foil of the the other, and the country would go to ruin speedily if either of these tendencies should be greatly weakened.

In our own political history we have generally found two contrasted policies arrayed against each other, in whose equilibrium the strength of our government is found. These are the policy of the centralization of power and the policy of the diffusion of power. There must be strength in the general government; much authority must be

given to Congress and to the national executive; the lack of that was what made the
old confederation a rope of sand, and led to
the adoption of the present Constitution : at
the same time, it is absolutely essential that
as many as possible of the interests of life
be committed directly to the people ; that
the principle of local self-government be
carefully cherished; that the people of each
state and of each local community be permitted to manage their own local affairs in
their own way. Thus we have the two policies of centralization and diffusion always
confronting each other. Some statesmen,
like Hamilton and Washington, see the defects of a weak central power very clearly,
and urge the strengthening of the national
government; others, like Jefferson and Pat-
rick Henry, are impressed by the evils of
centralized authority, and urge a wide diffusion of power. Both are right. The path
of wisdom for the nation is the middle
course. The safety and peace of the commonwealth is not found in canceling either

of these forces, but in strengthening both of them, and in holding the balance evenly between them.

In morals we find the same phenomenon. The foundation of Christian morality, as set forth in the command of Christ, " Thou shalt love thy neighbor as thyself," coördinates two principles, — self-love and benevolence, — what the philosophers call egoism and altruism. Thou shalt love thyself and thou shalt love thy neighbor, and these two loves shall be equal ; this is the substance of the Christian law. It is often supposed that Christianity forbids the love of self and requires an absolute self-abnegation, which may even involve the loss of one's own soul. The old Hopkinsian theology taught that one must be willing to be damned, in order that he might be saved. But this is not Christianity. That recognizes as of absolute worth every human soul, and enjoins upon every man to estimate his own manhood at the price which was paid for its redemption. Because I am a child of God, made in his image, I must highly value myself ; I must hold my own manhood in honor ; I must seek, in every lawful way, to develop its powers, to enlarge its capacities of knowledge and of happiness : to make it what God meant it to be. The love of self is therefore a fundamental obligation. But every other man is also a child of God, made in the same image, fitted for the same great services, the same ennobling joys ; and I must value the manhood of every other man as I value my own ; I must not seek my own welfare or happiness at the expense of any other man ; I must cherish the welfare and the happiness of every other man as I cherish my own ; I must love my neighbor as I love myself. Now the true morality does coördinate these two principles of self-love and benevolence. Neither of them has, or can have, in the heart of the perfectly moral man, any precedence over the other. The negation of either of them is the denial of morality.

Of course, there is a great deal of theorizing about morals, which does deny one or the other of them. The prevailing utilitarianism assumes that all virtue reduces to self-love; that right action is that which gives us greatest pleasure. Many modern philosophers unhesitatingly declare that egoism is the superior motive; that my personal welfare or happiness is the supreme consideration; and that though I may, in various refinements of egoism, come to act sometimes very much as if my motives were disinterested, yet that the deepest spring of all my conduct must always be self-love. For myself, I do not believe that this is morality at all; nor that any man with whom agreeable feeling or individual welfare is the dominant motive is a moral man, or knows what morality means. And it is not difficult to see that in proportion as this philosophy prevails, the very foundations of morality are undermined, and the flood-gates of vice and dissoluteness are flung open.

Nor is there, on the other hand, any sure basis for morality in the doctrine that makes altruism the sole and supreme principle of action, that enjoins a self-denial which ignores personal integrity and personal welfare. The outcome of that theory can be nothing but fanaticism. Sound morality rests exactly where Christ placed it, on the equivalence of self-love and benevolence. These two principles must be coördinated ; you cannot ignore either of them ; you cannot subordinate either of them ; you must hold them firmly together as the twin foundations of morality.

There is still another aspect of moral science in which we see the same duality of motive. When the question is raised respecting the factors of character, we hear two replies. There are those who say that circumstances make the man ; there are those who contend that the man's character is due to his personal force or weakness, and that circumstances have no control over character. Materialistic evolutionism regards the environment as responsible for nearly everything ; some schools of theological ethics practically ignore the environment, and lay

the whole responsibility upon individual
choice.   The truth is, that the two agencies
are all the while at work; that due account
must be taken of both; that it is very shal-
low and one-sided philosophy which neglects
or depreciates either of them.   Yet a good
share of the disputes about social reform that
are always filling the air arise from the fact
that some persons see one side of this question very clearly and refuse to see the other;
and about an equal number are equally
perverse in their determination to stand and
look on the opposite side of the shield.

The social troubles that are constantly
burdening our hearts, — the want and des-
titution among the working people, — what
is the cause of them?   It is the fault of
the political or the industrial system, say
some reformers.   It is unjust and burden-
some taxation; it is a bad organization
of labor; we must revolutionize the whole
social and political order; we must abolish
the tariff; we must levy all our taxes on the
land; we must nationalize all capital; it is

the environment that is at fault, we must change that ; that is the only remedy.   No, say another class, the government is all right ; taxation is fair enough ; the industrial organization is the best possible ; the trouble is with the working people themselves ; they are lazy, shiftless, wasteful, unreasonable ; if they would work for such wages as they can get and save what they earn, there would be little poverty.   Which is right ? Both are right, and both are wrong.   Government is at fault ; taxation is inequitable ; the industrial system, as based wholly on competition, is fundamentally defective. On the other side, many working people are lazy and inefficient and wasteful and impractical ; a large share of their miseries do come from this source.   Yet capitalists, as a class, will see nothing but the faults of the laborers ; and labor reformers and socialists, as a class, will see nothing but the faults of the present régime.   The well-to-do classes are inclined to insist that nothing shall be done until the laborers mend their ways ;

and the labor reformers and the socialists sometimes tell the workingman that he is a fool if he tries to improve his condition by being more industrious and more economical; that there is no cure except a radical reconstruction of society. And because of this stupid and half-idiotic, one-sided view of both parties, progress toward the amelioration of the social order is very slow. The environment does need mending, and so do the men; those of us who have something to do with the making of laws and the organization of industries are bound to do what we can to improve the environment; until we do that we have no right to scold the laboring man for his improvidence and inefficiency. The laboring man, on the other hand, is bound to correct his own faults; until he does, his outcries against the untoward circumstances will make but little impression.

In the temperance reform the same phenomenon confronts us. The prevailing temperance sentiment of the period puts the emphasis upon the environment; it is the environment that needs reforming, and not the men; we must remove temptation; we must shut up the saloons; that is the only cure for intemperance. This is the cry of the typical temperance man of the period. Over against him stand an army of men who declare that the environment has little or nothing to do with the case; that the only temperance reform that is of any value is the reformation of the habits of individuals; that when men stop drinking the saloon will be closed for want of patronage, and that that is the only way in which they ever will be closed. Now the truth is, that both these methods are necessary, and that they are equally necessary. We are bound to do what we can to improve the environment, to remove temptation; just as fast as it can be done, we are to shut up the saloons, and reduce the area of temptation; for the sake of the weaker members of society, who lack the moral stamina to resist temptation, these preventive measures must be resorted to. Society has a perfect right thus to protect itself against an acknowledged evil. No man's personal liberty to buy liquor on every street corner can be defended, when it is proved that the maintenance of this liberty involves the deterioration of public morality, and the imposing of a heavy burden of taxation upon honest industries. But this right and duty to deal sharply with the saloon power should never be urged (as it generally is urged) in such a way as to imply that the men who yield to existing temptations are practically guiltless; that so long as the saloons are open no man can be greatly blamed for making a beast of himself by the use of strong drink. I .think that the general tone of temperance discussion at the present day is utterly mischievous, because it does make just this impression, that the saloon is wholly responsible for the drunkenness of the period, and that the men who patronize the saloons are not responsible at all.

Passing to another phase of the temperance question, there are those who insist that drunkenness is a disease, and that it is not a sin; there are those who insist that it is a sin, and that it is not a disease. Both are wrong in what they deny, and right in what they affirm. It is a sin, and it is also, in many cases, a disease. Medical treatment is often necessary, and moral stimulus and restraint are equally necessary. The drunkard's disordered stomach and nerves must be treated therapeutically, and his enfeebled will and dulled conscience and damaged self-respect must be treated ethically. Any treatment which despises either of these methods is quackery.

Even insanity is now by the wisest alienists subjected to vigorous moral treatment, especially in its earlier stages. The doctors have found out that there are two sides to a man, and that when he is diseased it is folly and nonsense to expend all the effort upon one side of him and neglect the other. They put much emphasis upon the rousing of the patient's will, the strengthening of his self-control, the exercise of the rational and mental power which he still possesses.

It is undoubtedly true that the tendency has been very strong in modern medicine to neglect the spiritual and moral nature, to make no account whatever of this hemisphere of human life ; and this has led to the opposite extravagances of mind-cure and Christian science, and all that sort of thing, which, under one name or another, is all the while prevailing. But the mind-curers, on their part, are just as one-sided as the people over against them, who forget that man has a mind ; both sides of the man must be studied and wisely ministered unto ; it is ridiculous to suppose that you can cure all mental disorders with drugs and dietings, and equally ridiculous to suppose that you can cure all bodily disorders by thinking that they are cured, or praying that they may be.

These illustrations sufficiently set forth the principle under consideration. Those who consider them will be constrained to admit that many questions have two sides, and that those who wish to understand such questions must be willing to take a fair look at both sides.

The kind of dualism here suggested does not set one portion of the universe over against another in an irreconcilable conflict; it is only a diversity that is revealed in the progress toward unity. The " self " and the " not-self " are elementary and contrasted terms of thought; but the unity of the two is the presupposition of all thinking. So these contrasted phases of life are no irreducible antagonisms; each is essential to the integrity of the other; both are included in a higher unity. But every truly sane man must be able to comprehend this fact, that human progress is largely due to forces that limit and check each other, and thus, by their reactions, strengthen and support each other.

XI.

RULING IDEAS.

The Divine End, or final cause of all things, is the consummate and perfect life, of which Christ is the type. But this Divine Life is not an end outside the process of its development. It is immanent in the whole process, as the quickening and organizing principle of the whole. It is at once the end or consummation and the instrumental cause of the whole movement. . . . What we see in Christ is the Divine Life that has ever been immanent in the world, ever unfolding itself toward its perfect glory, as both the instrumental and the final cause of all things. — I. M. WHITON, *Gloria Patri*, page 59.

[The New Theology] holds that every man must live a life of his own, build himself up into a full personality, and give an account of himself to God: but it also recognizes the blessed truth that man's life lies in its relations; that it is a derived and shared life; that it is carried on and perfected under laws of heredity and of the family and the nation; that while he is "himself alone," he is also a son, a parent, a citizen, and an inseparable part of the human race. . . . It turns our attention to the corporate life of man here in the world, — an individual life, indeed, but springing from common roots, fed by a common life, watched over by one Father, inspired by one Spirit, and growing to one end; no man, no generation, being "made perfect" by itself. Hence its ethical emphasis; hence its recognition of the nation and of the family, and of social and commercial life, as fields of the manifestation of God and of the operation of the Spirit; hence its readiness to ally itself with all movements for bettering the condition of mankind, — holding that human society itself is to be redeemed, and that the world itself, in its corporate capacity, is being reconciled to God; hence, also, an apparently secular tone, which is, however, but a widening of the field of the divine and spiritual. — THEODORE T. MUNGER, *The Freedom of Faith*, page 25.

XI.

RULING IDEAS.

THE arguments and illustrations of the preceding chapters rest upon certain fundamental ideas which have been more or less clearly indicated from time to time, but which it may be well to bring together in the closing chapter.

The first is that doctrine of the immanence of the Christ, which was specially referred to in the fourth chapter. This great doctrine is clearly brought out in Paul's later epistles : the Epistle to the Ephesians, so called, and the Epistle to the Colossians. It is significant, as concerning the method of revelation, that this profound view of the Incarnation was not reached by the great Apostle until near the end of his ministry. To a vision purified by long fellowship with the Spirit and by the good discipline of trial this truth was vouchsafed.

Paul might not have been fitted, when he wrote his first letter to the Thessalonians, for the dispensation of this mystery. And even as the truth was one of the latest communicated to Paul, so it has been one of the latest to be received by the church. Indeed, it may be doubted whether the church could, before this generation, have made much use of this doctrine. The law of continuity is involved in it, and the application of this law to the physical order has but recently been naturalized in the popular conception. Men had to be made familiar with the idea of an orderly progress in creation, before they could get much benefit from the conception of Christianity as a normative germ or force planted in the very heart of the creation, and working itself out in the slow processes of history. The idea is not yet by any means familiar, yet flashes of its illuminating light are seen here and there in the dusk of time, pointing out the direction in which progress lies.[1]

[1] It is a striking fact that to a few of the Greek Fathers, to Clement of Alexandria especially, this truth was clearly made known.

I have spoken of the idea as Pauline ; but the author of the Fourth Gospel tells us that the Word was in the beginning with God, and that all things were made *through* Him ; that apart from Him nothing was made. This means that those attributes of God which are revealed to the world in Christ were the molds in which the whole creation was shaped ; that Christliness is the channel through which the creative energy of God has poured itself out from the beginning. This is the " mystery," the " stewardship " of which so pressed upon the spirit of the Apostle Paul, and which he so earnestly strove, in the epistles to the Ephesians and the Colossians, to " bring to light ; " — " the mystery which from all ages hath been hid in God who created all things ; " and the gospel, as he conceived of it, was proclaimed " to the intent that now unto the principalities and the powers in the heavenly places might be made known through the church the manifold wisdom of God according to the eternal purpose which he purposed in Christ Jesus our Lord." The eternal purpose, which was realized in Christ, is thus immediately connected with the act of creation ; and even " before the foundation of the world," as the Apostle says in another place, this purpose looked forward " unto a dispensation of the fullness of the times, to sum up all things in Christ, the things in the heavens and the things upon the earth." All this is made even more explicit in that passage of the Epistle to the Colossians, where Paul declares that Christ is " the first-born of all creation ; for *in Him were all things created*, in the heavens and upon the earth, things visible and things invisible, whether thrones or dominions or principalities or powers ; all things have been created *through* Him, and unto Him ; and He is before all things, and in Him all things consist." Not only the physical creation, but the social order also, finds its *raison d'être* in the Christ. Thrones and dominions, as well as genera and species, are explained by Him. The law of the spirit of life in Christ Jesus is the law of the universe. It is the unity which springs from love, not less than the unity which is the postulate of reason, that makes it a universe.

It would be difficult to frame statements in which this great truth of the immanence of Christ in the very structure of the natural world and of the social world could be more definitely set forth than it is here set forth by the Apostle Paul ; and it would be quite as difficult to conceive of any truth of revelation more momentous. Surely, it puts a new face upon nature, and gives us a wholly new conception of life and duty. The whole world is transfigured by the conception. To find the very attributes of God which are manifested in Christ incorporated into the order of creation, and slowly unveiling themselves to the sight of men ; to learn, by the study of life upon this planet, that love, in the forms of sympathy and self-sacrifice, are parts of His ways by whom the worlds were made, — is to get a new view of the meaning of life.

It is true that the doctrine of the immanence of God has become quite familiar in
recent years. Since the day of Benedict
Spinoza, the carpenter theory of creation
has been greatly discredited, and the presence of God in his world has been generally
admitted. The fear of pantheism has not
been permitted to dig an impassable chasm
between the Creator and the creation. That
"series of antitheses between the universe
and God, in time, in space, in causation, in
excellence," of which Dr. Martineau speaks,
the tendency of which, as he says, " is to
overshadow the world by the contrast of a
transcendent glory, and to depress it with
a conscious insignificance," is no longer the
habit of Christian thought. That ancient
deism is a waning philosophy. And all
that the same writer has to say about this
old conception is worth heeding : " The
sense of ephemeral life, of overwhelming
law, of hurrying death, of twilight knowledge, and only fancied power, settles upon
the heart of such a faith, and drives it upon

artifices of self-relief. The provinces of the
natural and the supernatural are sharply
marked off from one another, in date, in
seat, in agency: the former belonging to
second causes, to the cosmic interlude, and
the scene of physical existence ; the latter to
the action of the First Cause, before, after,
and outside the regular ordering of the
world ; so that the supernatural can never
be human, and the natural, except in its
first institution, can never be divine. In
short, the legislating mind of the universe
and its executive media are kept separate
from each other; the one an imperative
prefix that 'spake and it was done ; ' the
others, constant servitors, engaged with
purely ministerial functions unconsciously
performed. What is present with us and
around us is only mechanism, running down
through its appointed term; and for any
such freshly moving will as is needed for
personal relations, we must look, in one direction, further than the dawn of geologic
time, and, in the other, to the ' unseen uni-

verse,' beyond the equalization of heat and
the death of all things in this." [1]   This conception answers none of the purposes of religion ; we must have a God to worship and
to trust in who is nearer at hand than this ;
and therefore, without going over into the
other extreme of pantheism, the faith of the
Christian church has been hopefully feeling after that God whom Paul preached to
the Athenians, in whom we live and move
and have our being.   The tendency of
thought of which Wordsworth was the great
exponent has taken possession of the Christian consciousness ; and the truth that nature is to us the constant revelation of the
presence and power of God is beginning to
be a reality.

Nevertheless, the revelation of God in
nature has been accepted as only partial.
Nature, it has been supposed, makes known
to us God as law.   His power, his wisdom,
perhaps, also, to some extent, his benevolence may be inferred from the things that

[1] A Study of Religion, ii. 144.

are made ; but the deeper truths of the Incarnation and the Redemption are not, as we
have been taught, even suggested to us in
nature. Indeed, Christianity, as a system,
has been assumed to be wholly separate from
the natural order, and even set over against
it in contrast; nature and grace are anti-
thetical terms.

To one who holds this view of the Christian system, the doctrine of the immanence
of the Christ must come with something of
a shock. No doubt, it will require the re-
consideration and the reversal of some of his
stock notions ; and those to whom the summons " Change your minds " is unwelcome,
will not entertain it. But it is an important
question, after all, whether this doctrine, so
clearly taught by Paul and John, is not the
very deepest truth of the Bible ; whether it
is not the fundamental fact of creation and
of revelation ; and if it is, the effort to ad-
just to it our conceptions of life and duty
cannot be regarded as too onerous. We
have a great deal to do with this world in

which we live ; it is the school in which our
characters are trained, and everything depends upon our learning its primary lessons.
If the truth of which Jesus the Christ is the
manifestation did not first appear in the
world about nineteen hundred years ago ; or
if it was not first adumbrated in certain ritual observances prescribed a few centuries
earlier ; if, on the contrary, it was the very
theme of the song of the morning stars when
they sang together ; if it begins to find its
expression in the lowest orders of living
creatures ; if the rudiments of love and self-
sacrifice, — the elements of Christliness, —
are among the primordial tendencies of
nature ; and if these principles have been
steadily developing since the beginning of
creation, so that what was first a mere unconscious tendency has emerged into an
ethical law, — then our religion has a footing
and a sanction in this world which the world
has not hitherto confessed. If all this is so,
then what new and large meaning is given
to the thought of Christ as one who comes,

not to destroy but to fulfill the law, and to
bring life as well as immortality to light.
It is the law of life that he fulfills and illu-
minates. If this is so, all life is sacramental and revelatory ; " the struggle for the
life of others," which appears in the lowest
tribes, is the proof that in the Christ of Cal-
vary all things consist and become intelligible. If this is so, then He through whom
all things were made " came to his own " in
a deeper sense than we have given to the
words, when He stood among us, pointing
to the fowls of the air and considering the
lilies.

"To look reverently at the face of nature
is to look into the face of Christ. We see
his lineaments as through a veil, but He is
there. By the mystery of his human birth
and ours we know that He has been, nay,
that He *is*, in this vast, visible, unfolding of
invisible being, with us, — spirit revealed
through form.

"There is a conscious being somewhere
behind every unconscious manifestation of

life, or it could never have existed at all. We call it the working of a spirit. What spirit? Is there any other source of life than the one spirit, — God? Is there more than one God, — He who is known to us as Father, Son, and Spirit, — the One Life? And can we divide his nature, and say that by this part of himself He gives this kind of life, and by that, another? Has He no human interest in the place He has prepared for his human family, even though it be only their temporary residence?"

" No; we shall never understand nature, except in a manner entirely superficial, until we look into her spirit with spiritual eyes, like Christ's, — the only true human vision. For the habitation of man, as well as his form, is shaped by the Spirit and planned by the Father and the Son from the beginning. 'By whom He made all worlds.' 'All things were made through Him, and apart from Him was not anything made that was made.'" [1]

[1] *The Unseen Friend*, by Lucy Larcom, pp. 159, 160.

Another of the truths assumed in the foregoing chapters is the truth that the relations of men to one another in society are not contractual, but vital and organic; that we are members one of another; that no man reaches perfection or happiness apart from his fellow-men; that no man liveth to himself, and none dieth to himself. This conception of the organic unity of society has been more or less familiar; indeed, it could hardly be ignored by those who had Paul's epistles in their hands: but the assumption of interpreters has been that these figures of Paul represented the society of the regenerate, — the organized church; and that no such relations were to be looked for outside the ecclesiastical pale. By this limitation the whole force of the idea has been dissipated. If these vital relations subsist only between those who have passed through some transcendental experience, and are no part of the common heritage of humanity, mankind in general will not be able to take any deep interest in them.

It ought to be remembered, however, by interpreters who insist on giving these analogies of Paul a purely ecclesiastical reference, that Paul was describing the Christian society rather than any mere ecclesiasticism; and that, in Paul's conception, the Christian society was destined to become universal; the day was coming when every knee should bow and every tongue confess that Christ was Lord. And the relations thus established would be the normal relations among men. If men as Christians were to become members one of another, it was only because as men they were made to be members one of another. This manner of living together was not something imported into humanity by Christ; it was only the realization, by his grace, of the ideal of humanity. For even as the Christian is not something other than the perfect type of humanity, but the restoration of that type, so the Christian society is nothing other than the perfect human society, the society which unfallen and sinless human beings would spontaneously form.

To limit Paul's figure of the body with many members to the church is, therefore, grievously to belittle a great truth. Christ is the head of the church, but he is also the head of humanity; and the true relation of every human being to the race is that of the member to the body. To every man, whether within or without the church, this truth needs to be brought home. No man comprehends life until he is made to see by how many organic filaments he is bound to his fellows; how utterly impossible it is for him to separate his interests and his fortunes from theirs; in how many ways the welfare of those who are round about him depends upon the working, in due measure, of that part of the organism which he is.

" Wondrous, truly," cries Herr Teufelsdroeckh, "are the bonds that unite us one and all; whether by the soft binding of Love or the iron chain of Necessity, as we like to choose it. More than once have I said to myself of some perhaps whimsically strutting Figure, such as provokes whimsical thoughts, ' Wert thou, my little Brotherkin, suddenly covered up within the largest imaginable Glass bell, — what a thing it were, not for thyself only, but for the world! Post Letters, more or fewer, from all the four winds, impinge upon thy Glass walls, but must drop unread ; neither from within comes there question or response into any post-bag ; thy Thoughts fall into no friendly ear or heart, thy Manufacture into no purchasing hand ; thou art no longer a circulating venous-arterial Heart, that, taking and giving, circulatest through all Space and all Time ; there has a Hole fallen out in the immeasurable universal World-tissue, which must be darned up again.' Such venous-arterial circulation of Letters, verbal Messages, paper and other Packages, going out from him and coming in, a blood circulation, visible to the eye ; but the finer nervous circulation, by which all things, the minutest that he does, minutely influence all men, and the very look of his face blesses or curses whomso it lights on, and so generates ever new blessing or new cursing, — all this you cannot see but only imagine." [1]

One more ruling idea, which the preceding chapters imply, is the presence of the kingdom of God. That this kingdom is to come in larger measure, with wider dominion and more pervasive control, is the faith and the prayer of every true disciple; but it is also his assurance that the kingdom is here; that all its essential forces are now in active operation; that righteousness and peace and joy in the Holy Ghost are not to be awaited, because they have come, with all their blessed influences, to dwell among us; that the love which is the fulfilling of the law is just as truly regnant in the world to-day as it ever will be in heaven : not so widely regnant, indeed, but not less truly. The reality is here; its completion is yet to come. Few lives are yet wholly under its influence; few homes are completely ruled by its pure precept; few institutions perfectly

[1] *Sartor Resartus*, Book III. ch. vii.

obey its royal law: yet its benign sway is felt, in some degree, in innumerable places; its pervasive force, like the leaven, is at work everywhere; it is as silent as light, as subtle as life, and mightier than either. The thought of the world is gradually being freed from superstition and prejudice; the social sentiments are being purified; the customs are slowly changing for the better; the laws are gradually shaped by finer conceptions of justice. There are reactions and disasters, but taking the ages together the progress is sure. God is in his world; He has never yet departed from it, nor can we conceive of Him as withdrawing, for one moment, his presence or his control. He is not in haste. A thousand years in his sight are but as yesterday when it is past, and as a watch in the night. As the husbandman waiteth for the precious fruit of the earth, being patient over it, so the Eternal waiteth for the reaping of his great purposes. But his days go on, and his designs fail not.

" The slow, sweet hours that bring us all things good,
  The slow, sad hours that bring us all things ill,
    And all good things from evil "

are the servitors of his throne. And his victorious love is steadily leading on the generations to that far-off divine event which our strongest faith but imperfectly discerns. The presence in the world of mighty forces of evil, of principalities and powers of darkness, is not to be gainsaid : but the kingdom does not belong to them ; it never did, and it never will. The kingdom of the world is become the kingdom of our Lord and of his Christ, and He shall reign for ever and ever.

The conception of this kingdom of God as something future — as a reign yet to be set up on the earth — has been derived from an extremely literalistic reading of those glowing texts that describe the great accessions of power which are yet to come, from time to time, to the empire of our King. One can easily believe that there are to be, perhaps in days not distant, marvelous forward movements of the forces of the kingdom. The social conditions seem even now to be preparing for a revelation to the world of the glory of Christ, which shall be overpowering in its splendor, — like the lightning which cometh forth from the east and is seen even unto the west. But these great manifestations of his royalty will be only the fuller unfolding of truths which are here in the world to-day. A few men in the world believe that the law of love is the law of all life, and that nothing else will give us peace and prosperity. Suppose that, as the result of social struggles and overturnings, this truth should be so enforced upon the minds of the great multitude of employers and employed that they could not doubt it; and suppose that there should be a world-wide movement to substitute goodwill for greed as the organizing principle of industrial society : such an event as that might be described as the coming of Christ to the world with power and great glory; none of the apocalyptic emblems would overstate its dramatic significance. And yet it would be simply the wider acceptance, by the world, of a law which is now recognized and established among men.

The point to be noted is that the kingdom is here, a kingdom still increasing; and that the coming which we pray for can be nothing more than the fuller development and manifestation of the blessed life which now, in so many places, and by so many heavenly ministries, is making the earth beautiful and glad.

How, now, must our personal conceptions of life and duty be affected by the apprehension of these great truths? It must be evident, in a moment, that the Christian disciple, to whom the relation of Christ to the world is only that of an architect; to whom the relations of men to one another in society are those of voluntary contract; and to whom the coming of the kingdom of heaven is a wholly future event, to follow the destruction of the present social order, — must have a very different conception of personal

life and duty from that which is entertained
by one who finds in the life of the world
about him the revelation of the love of
Christ; who feels that, without any choice
of his own, every human being is vitally related to him, and who knows that the kingdom of heaven, a silently growing but irresistible dominion, is here in the world to-day.
The immanence of Christ, the vital unity of
the race, the presence of the kingdom, —
these truths give to life a new sacredness,
and to duty new cogency. The artificiality
and formalism with which the old conceptions were invested give place to naturalness and reality. Christianity is no longer
anti-natural; it is in the deepest sense natural. We may claim that its profoundest
laws, including its law of sacrifice, may
be inductively verified. We are not following cunningly devised fables when we
proclaim the truth as it is in Jesus; we are
laying hold upon the everlasting verities.
Humanity is the crown of the creation,
and Christ is the head of humanity. The

man Christ Jesus completes and explains the revelation that began with the beginning of the creation. We stand on solid ground to proclaim the gospel of his grace. "Nature," says one, "is ever the counterpart of our Lord. The temporal hath no strife with the eternal. Like the union of soul and body is the union of the heavenly with the earthly, of the endless life of the kingdom with our mortal life. It is only as our Lord reviveth in our hearts the spiritual meanings of nature and of the kingdom that we have the full revelation of the Father; and, abiding in Him as He abideth in the Father, we have, even in this earthly existence, everlasting life, being associated with Him in coöperation with the eternal purposes of an infinite love." [1]

The doctrine of the immanence of the Christ makes the old distinction between the sacred and the secular meaningless and almost blasphemous. All life is sacred. What

[1] *God in His World*, p. 177.

God hath cleansed by the indwelling Word, that call not thou common or unclean.

Nor can we allow Mr. Kidd's contention that the Christian morality is ultra-rational. It is only to a philosophy which is semi-rational that it bears any such look. Take in all the facts, and the Christian altruism is scientifically verified. The morality of strife is based upon an incomplete induction. If the race is one body with many members, if there is but one life and one law, that law must be love. To one who admits the organic unity of the human race, the notion that Christ's law is ultra-rational is absurd. It is and must be the law of the organism. It is the simple scientific expression of the relation of the members to the body. The bond that unites us to our fellows is, therefore, one that we cannot sunder. To sever ourselves from our kind is self-mutilation. This is not some counsel of perfection for saints ; it is the fundamental fact of life. All our industry, all our social organization, must conform to it. No man

liveth unto himself. Our daily work is a
social function. Wealth is valueless and
impossible apart from human fellowship.
Not to keep this steadily before us in our
administration of all our affairs is to be
false to the primary human obligation. To
set up natural law in the social world or
the business world, as distinct from and
contrary to the Christian law, is not only
unmoral, it is unscientific. Love is the
fulfilling of all law. And not only do these
ideas make our life sacred and love our
daily regimen, they ought to fill us also
with confidence and courage. The kingdom
that we pray for and fight for is not a mere
hope, it is a solid reality. When we say
that we are working together with God, we
know what we mean. We can discern his
working, and can be confident that we are
helping in the fulfillment of his great designs. The signs of his presence and power
are everywhere. The victories that He has
won over the powers of darkness and cruelty
and greed are more than we can number.

The social philosopher, scanning the tendencies which he finds in history, declares that "it is possible to follow through the centuries the progress of a revolution unequaled in magnitude and absolutely unique in character, a revolution the significance of which is perceived to lie not, as is so often supposed, in its tendency to bring about a condition of society in which the laws of previous development are to be suspended, but in the fact that it constitutes the last orderly stage in the same cosmic process which has been in the world from the beginning of life."[1] This mighty movement, the same philosopher tells us, is identified with the Christian religion. It is the kingdom of heaven which Christ proclaimed, into which is gathered the harvest of the centuries, and by which the kingdoms of this world are being subdued to righteousness. To those who have intelligently allied themselves with this kingdom, and are seeking its righteousness, doubt is an absurdity and fear a sole-

[1] *Social Evolution*, p. 148.

cism. Repulses and disasters can seem to them but temporary reverses; the future is secure. They strive not nor cry; they haste not nor rest; for the eternal God is their dwelling-place, and underneath them are the everlasting arms.